THE EASTERN CATHOLIC LITURGIES

THE EASTERN CATHOLIC LITURGIES

A Study in Words and Pictures

Text by Rev. N. Liesel

Photographs by T. Makula

Foreword by Donald Attwater

The Newman Press
Westminster • Maryland
1960

Nihil obstat: EDWARD A. CERNY, S.S., S.T.D.
Censor Librorum

Imprimatur: FRANCIS P. KEOUGH, D.D.
Archbishop of Baltimore

May 11, 1960

To
Our Eastern Brethren

Roma, April 6, 1956
Via della Conciliazione, 34

SACRA CONGREGATIO
"PRO ECCLESIA ORIENTALI"

PROT. NUM. 182/56

This valuable volume on the Eastern Catholic Liturgies presents an account of the normal mode of celebrating the Holy Sacrifice of the Altar, or the Divine Liturgy as it is more properly called, by Catholics of the various Eastern rites. It illustrates well the nature and characteristics of the Eucharistic Action as seen in the prayers and ceremonies of the liturgical office in the various traditions of the different ritual groups. The photographs accompanying the text have been carefully chosen to give Western Catholics a closer acquaintance with the Liturgy of each of the Oriental rites.

The prayers of the various Liturgies, which have come down to us from the very earliest Christian centuries, are imbued with sturdy piety. The profundity of their symbolism and the wealth of their theological teaching make them invaluable for the devotion and edification of Christians of every tradition.

It is my sincere hope that this book may enrich the understanding and devotion of Catholics, Eastern and Western alike, and may serve to deepen and strengthen their mutual esteem for one another. May it also serve to show those brethren of ours still separated from us that in the unity of faith and obedience the Church has no desire to deprive them of a single item of their ancient and noble heritage, and that from their union with us there would come no alteration in their legitimate liturgical observances. This book gives ample proof of the fact that when liturgical variations have set in among Eastern groups in union with the Holy See, it is the express wish of the Church that efforts be made in the direction of restoration of their ancient purity.

I earnestly invoke God's blessing on this work, and hope that it will enjoy the wide circulation it merits.

+ Eugenio Card. Tisserant
seg.:

A. Coussa
ass.

FOREWORD

During the past twenty-five years English versions have been published of the ordinary parts of the eucharistic Liturgy (Mass) of all the Catholic Eastern rites; of the principal one, the Byzantine Liturgy, English translations have, indeed, been numerous. But for the purpose of getting an idea of the "look" and "feel" of a religious service, a printed text, though necessary, does not get one very far: as the author of this book says in his preface, "an ounce of seeing is worth a pound of reading." The obvious thing to do is to attend an actual celebration in a church; but for most English-speaking people this is easier said than done. In Great Britain or Australia, for example, Catholic refugees or other immigrants have some churches of their own rite, mostly Slav-Byzantine, but they are very few and far between; and even in the United States and Canada, where such churches are relatively numerous, they are nevertheless somewhat localized: it is easy enough to worship at an Eastern Liturgy in Pennsylvania, but not in Texas or California.

It is therefore for us a specially happy idea of Father N. Liesel to provide an album of annotated photographs, which supplement printed texts but are at the same time valuable for their own sake. The photographs in this book include moments from all the Eastern eucharistic Liturgies as celebrated by Christians in communion with Rome; namely, those of the *Alexandrian rite* in its Coptic and Ethiopian forms; the *Antiochene rite* in its (Pure) Syrian, Malankarese and Maronite forms; the *Byzantine rite,* according to Greek, Melkite, Russian and Ruthenian (Ukrainian) usages; the *Chaldean* or *East Syrian rite* in its Chaldean and Malabarese forms; and the Liturgy of the *Armenian rite.*

These striking photographs were all taken in Rome, and in that there is a fine symbolic significance: all this human variety in ways of celebrating the eucharistic Sacrifice gathered together at the heart of the Church, where it is never forgotten that "The Church of Jesus Christ is neither Latin nor Greek nor Slav—she is Catholic" (Pope Benedict XV). But the fact that they were taken in Italy has this drawback, that necessarily many of the photographs could not be taken in churches built and furnished according to the relevant rite. In addition, it meant that there could be no pictures of typical congregations, the people of God for and with whom the Sacrifice is being offered. It is sometimes overlooked that the distinguishing characteristics of a Liturgy do not begin and end with what goes on at and around the altar. These points matter less than they might have done, however, since most of the pictures are "close-ups" of the celebrating priest.

Especially since Pope Leo XIII, the Holy See has been insistent that the Catholic Eastern churches should observe their proper rites and customs without modification, and has taken great trouble to publish authentic texts. But to anyone with some little knowledge of these matters, the pictures in this book are clear evidence that (quite apart from the special cases of the Maronites and Malabarese) the elimination of liturgical hybridism is far from finished yet: leavened altarbreads that approximate to unleavened wafers, Western altar-linen, such as the corporal and the pall, lacey albs instead of *stikharia*, stiff gestures and carriage of the hands by celebrant and ministers, and so on. Small things, apparently, and concerned with minor external matters; but they have significance for the integrity of a rite, which means much more than formulas alone, as Pope Pius XII made abundantly clear. And they are part of a real obstacle to Christian understanding: non-Catholic Easterners are quick to detect and criticize such innovations. It can hardly be denied that nowadays there is need sometimes for a shortened and simplified form of celebration of a given Eastern Liturgy, at any rate in some places; but it is startling to read references in the text of Father Liesel's book to *silent* low Masses in certain rites.

Of the dozen priests photographed, half have so far departed from their own tradition as to be clean-shaven (particularly surprising in the Melkite and Chaldean priests). Nevertheless one is confronted by some strikingly beautiful faces among them, old and young. It is a reminder of how impressed the English Bishop Ullathorne was by the Eastern bishops at the Vatican Council: he wrote of "their movements and gestures quiet and gentle, full of dignity and self-possession," and of the young Armenian archbishop who "so irresistibly strikes me as exactly like our idea of our Lord."

An American correspondent recently wrote that "I fear that the Eastern rites are becoming the vogue [in this country], and therefore many people are missing the main points. Too many Latin Catholics believe that we are merely tolerating these beautiful and ancient rites of the Church." To whatever extent this may be true of North America, it is not surprising, for it is the same in some other lands. It is perhaps to be expected that Western Catholics, being in so huge a numerical majority and generally knowing nothing of other Catholic traditions, should assume that their own ways are the only "really Catholic ways," that they are necessarily superior, and that other ways are merely tolerated. This is especially so when the other ways are not only different from Western practice but the contrary of it, e.g., communion in both kinds (*species*) or the ordination of married men to the priesthood. But such an attitude is grievously mistaken. It was Pope Leo XIII, in *Orientalium dignitas,* who particularly emphasized that all rites are equal; it was Pope Pius XII who again assured Eastern Christians, whether Catholic or other, that "they will never have to exchange their own legitimate rites and ancient institutions for Latin rites and institutions: both are to be regarded with equal esteem and reverence . . ." (*Orientalis ecclesiae,* 1944).

In other words, uniformity is no part of the Catholic tradition: the Church's faith is the same always and everywhere, the ideals of Christian life are the same for all the faithful, always and everywhere; but in everything else there can be endless variety, for there is endless variety in human beings and peoples, in their institutions and cultures. The numerical degree of variety in the Church today is very much less than in the past, for historical reasons; it will become very much more again in the day, however far off it may be, when Catholics and non-Catholics are again united in the one Church of Jesus Christ. It is a common mistake to confuse uniformity with unity. For a number of people to have similar institutions and to do things in the same way is quite compatible with a gross state of disunity among those people, as we see all around us. But unity rises above all accidental variations, and embraces all differences that are not in themselves incompatible with unity. Uniformity merely makes people resemble one another; it is being and doing as parts of a whole that gives them unity, makes them one in the community whose governing principle is the Holy Spirit.

In somewhat the same way, the Mass is one but the ways of celebrating it are many, and always have been. That aspect of Catholic diversity-in-unity is as obvious and striking as it is important, and it is emphasized for us pictorially in Father Liesel's book. But it is far from being the only aspect, as was shown so admirably by an American Benedictine, Dom Polycarp Sherwood, writing on "The Sense of Rite" in the *Eastern Churches Quarterly,* vol. xii, no. 4, 1957-58 (C.N.E.W.A., New York; The Newman Bookshop, Oxford, and also in *Unitas,* Autumn 1957, Graymoor, N. Y.); that article is an excellent beginning for anyone who wants to go a bit below the surface of things.

But we all of us, students or not, ought to learn something about our fellow Catholics of rites different from our own, so far as our circumstances will allow; and the first way of doing this is to worship with them. And the best way of doing that is sometimes to go to Mass in their churches when opportunity offers. It must be emphasized, however, that we must not go just as spectators and sightseers, or to listen to the singing, but to join in the offering of the one Sacrifice. Obviously this cannot be done satisfactorily without first getting some idea of the text of the service, and for the Byzantine rite the following translations may be suggested: Russian usage, *The Byzantine Liturgy* (The Russian Center, Fordham, N. Y.); Ukrainian usage, *Christ With Us* (Ukrainian Seminary, Stamford, Conn.); Carpatho-Ruthenian usage, *The Divine Liturgy* (St. Procopius Abbey, Lisle, Ill.); Melkite usage, *Byzantine Missal* (St. George's Church, Birmingham, Ala.). But any one of these books is to a very large extent equally useful for a celebration in any Byzantine church.

In addition to the words of the Liturgy, study this book of Father Liesel's, not only the pictures but the text as well. There is a very great deal to be learned from it. The whole book is an impressive testimony to the real catholicity of the Church, and to the great variety of forms into which the simple actions and words of the Last Supper developed in neighbouring lands. It is a salutary reminder, too, that the Church was born in the East and her early growth and decisive development were there. And here the closing words of Father Sherwood's article, referred to above, are very relevant: "The human cultures entering into the formation of the Byzantine and Latin rites are closely akin; the basic forms of the Syrian culture belong to another world."

Donald Attwater

PREFACE

More than a quarter of a century ago, when I was still a student at the Pontifical Oriental Institute in Rome, I was gripped by the desire to make better known in the Western world the riches of the Church's Eastern heritage, and most especially the Eastern liturgies.

There is no lack of publications on this subject, but I felt that an ounce of seeing is worth a pound of reading; and the general public in the West did not and still does not ordinarily have an opportunity to see the liturgy celebrated in the various rites.

I therefore finally decided to make as full a collection of photographs as possible of the celebration of the Church's Eastern liturgies. I eventually succeeded in obtaining a complete photographic record of the Eucharistic liturgy of each of the twelve Eastern rites—more than a thousand photographs in all. These were produced by L. Schumacher, Erkenschwick in Westphalia, Germany, in the form of films (one for each liturgy) accompanied by an explanatory commentary.

It was unfortunately impossible to publish so large a mass of photographs in book form, but a representative selection of them was published, along with a brief account of each rite, in Germany in 1956; a second edition appeared in 1959.

I now have the pleasure of offering a translation of that work to the English-speaking public in the hope that it will contribute, in an immediate sense, to a knowledge of Eastern Christianity and, more remotely, to the longed-for union of the Christian Churches.

N. Liesel

CONTENTS

Letter from His Eminence, Eugene Cardinal Tisserant vii

Foreword ix

Preface xiii

Introduction xvii

   I. The Coptic Liturgy 3

  II. The Ethiopic Liturgy 17

 III. The Syrian Liturgy 31

 IV. The Malankarese Liturgy 48

  V. The Maronite Liturgy 61

 VI. The Greek Liturgy 77

 VII. The Melkite Liturgy 91

VIII. The Russian Liturgy 103

 IX. The Ruthenian Liturgy 117

  X. The Chaldean Liturgy 129

 XI. The Malabarese Liturgy 143

 XII. The Armenian Liturgy 155

INTRODUCTION

During the first centuries of its existence, Christianity developed a considerable number of popular forms of solemn public worship.

The first Christians—i.e., the Apostles, their followers, and their communities —celebrated the memory of the Lord, in the first instance, in a service of intercession and Scriptural readings which drew heavily upon the usages of the Jewish synagogue. The selection of readings from Holy Scripture, the prayers and ceremonies, were not at all rigidly ordered. It was only the actual Sacrifice and the Sacrificial Banquet which were probably celebrated according to certain established rubrics. But even these were elastic enough to permit, in the course of time, various forms to grow out of them.

After the establishment of the Patriarchates, the predominant liturgy of each was declared obligatory in that area. Thus there developed in each Patriarchate a certain rite, first in Greek, then in the vernacular.

Later on, doctrinal disputes concerning the nature and person of Christ occasioned still greater differences within the rites. Nationalistic and heterodox groups broke away from what was at that time the Catholic State Religion, whose Eastern center was Byzantium, and formed their own ecclesiastical communities with their own special customs. Such were, e.g., the Monophysites in Syria and Egypt, and the Nestorians in Persia.

A large part of the Syrians (Jacobites), Armenians (Gregorians), Copts (Egyptians), and Ethiopians went over to Monophysitism. They all remoulded the liturgy in their own way. Some of the Syrians (namely, the Maronites) used, until 1181, formulas rejected by the Council of Constantinople (681). They, too, developed their own rite.

The faithful of Syria and Egypt, who remained true to the Catholic or orthodox, i.e., "right-believing" (the sense given to the word until the eleventh century) State Church, were decried and reviled by the dissidents as Melkites (Royalists). These Melkites conserved for a long time the ancestral liturgies of the respective Patriarchates; but later, they began to accept the rite of the Imperial City, i.e., the Byzantine Liturgy. This process of acceptance was not completed till the thirteenth century.

Eventually five main rites developed: the Syrian, Alexandrine, Chaldean, Armenian, and Byzantine. To the Byzantine rite belong the Melkite, the Rumanian, the Slavonic, and several other rites. To the Syrian belong the Maronite and the Malankarite; to the Alexandrine, the Coptic and the Ethiopian. A special form of the Chaldean is the Malabarese.

Varied as these Christian rites may be in language, chant, and rubric, the basic pattern of the Mass is nonetheless the same in all liturgies:

1. the Eucharistic Prayers and Readings [Homiletic Liturgy];
2. the Eucharistic Sacrifice;
3. the Eucharistic Sacrificial Banquet.

From this fundamental unity, there evolved a marvelous variety of liturgical forms.

The Catholic Church fosters and prizes this treasure of primitive piety and permits her priests of various rites to celebrate Holy Mass daily in twelve different languages (Latin, Greek, Syriac, Armenian, Coptic, Geez Ethiopian, Georgian, Old Slavonic, and such modern languages as Rumanian, Hungarian, Arabic, Malayalam Indian [and English]).

THE ORIENTAL PATRIARCHATES

The four Patriarchates arose quite naturally in the capitals of the East: Alexandria, Antioch, Constantinople (Byzantium), and Jerusalem.

The Patriarchate of Alexandria comprised the Egyptian Provinces; that of Antioch, the Syrian. At the Council of Chalcedon (451), there came into being the Patriarchate of Constantinople consisting of three Exarchates: Heraclea in Thrace, Ephesus in Asia, and Caesarea in Pontus. The Patriarchate of Jerusalem was likewise established at this Council; it consisted of three ecclesiastical provinces in the southern part of the Patriarchate of Antioch.

Outside the territory of these four Patriarchates, there developed independently the Catholicate (Patriarchate) of Georgia, the Catholicate of Armenia, and the Catholicate of Chaldea of Persia, with the Malabar Indians subject to it.

Doctrinal differences brought about the establishment, within the territory of the Patriarchate of Antioch, of two rival patriarchates, the Jacobite and the Maronite; within the territory of the Patriarchate of Alexandria, of the dissident Coptic Patriarchate of Egypt and Ethiopia.

The Oriental Churches all broke away in time either from the unity of faith (thus becoming heretical) or from Primacy of the Catholic Church (thus becoming schismatic). Since the Middle Ages, however, individuals and groups have returned to the Catholic Church: in 1181 all the Maronites re-established contact with Rome; in 1550, some of the Chaldeans; in 1600, the Ruthenians; in 1725, the Melkites in Syria; in 1740, the Armenians and Copts; in 1930, the Malankarese returned to union with Rome. All these had or were granted their own hierarchies and Patriarchates, who are directly subject to the Pope in Rome. These Catholic Oriental Churches, therefore, are within the unity of the Roman Catholic Church.

ORGANIZATION OF THE EASTERN CATHOLIC CHURCHES

1. The Melkite Catholic Patriarchate of Alexandria, Antioch, and Jerusalem, united in the person of the Patriarchate of Antioch.
   (Residence: Damascus; during winter, Cairo)
2. The Armenian Catholic Patriarchate of Antioch
   (Residence: Beirut)
3. The Syro-Maronite Catholic Patriarchate of Antioch
   (Residence: Beirut-Bkerke)
4. The Syro-Malankarese Catholic Metropolitanate of Trivandrum
   (Residence: Trivandrum, India)
5. The Syro Catholic Patriarchate of Antioch
   (Residence: Beirut)
6. The Chaldean Catholic Patriarchate of Babylon
   (Residence: Bagdad)
7. The Chaldean-Malabarese Catholic Metropolitanate of Ernaculam
   (Residence: Ernaculam, India)
8. The Coptic Catholic Patriarchate of Alexandria
   (Residence: Cairo)
9. Two Ethiopian Catholic Exarchates:
   a. Addis Ababa for Ethiopia (Residence: Addis Ababa)
   b. Asmara for Eritrea (Residence: Asmara)
10. Byzantine Catholic (or Greek Catholic) communities: Albanians, Bulgarians, Greeks, Italo-Albanians, Yugoslavs, Rumanians, Ukrainians, White-Russians, Russians, Hungarians, Georgians. They are subject to the Sacred Congregation for the Oriental Church in Rome.

STATISTICS ON EASTERN CATHOLIC CHURCHES

	1951*	1960†
Chaldeans	141,000	195,953 (1959)
Malabarese	947,000	1,377,398 (1959)
Syrian	71,000	87,336 (1959)
Malankarese	60,000	108,092 (1959)
Copts	63,000	80,580 (1959)
Ethiopians	35,000	50,103 (1959)
Armenians	100,000	*c.* 100,000 (1959)
Maronites	366,000	533,459 (1959)
Byzantine		
Albanians	some	4,400 (1940)
Bulgarians	6,000	7,000 (1950)
Greeks	3,000	2,549 (1959)
Italo-Albanians	70,000	64,400 (1959)
Yugoslavs	43,000	56,350 (1959)
Melkites	170,000	229,488 (1959)
Rumanians	1,500,000	1,562,980 (1949)
Georgians		*c.* 50,000
Ruthenians (Ukrainians and White-Russians)		
in U.S.S.R.	5,202,400	4,025,220 (1944)
in Czechoslovakia		320,069 (1949)
in U.S.A.		483,074 (1959)
in Canada		221,448 (1959)
in Brazil		130,000 (1959)
in Argentina		100,000 (1959)
Russians abroad	3,000	*c.* 3,000 (1948)
Hungarians	142,000	195,440 (1948)
Totals (approximate)	8,922,400	9,988,339

* From De Vries, *Der christliche Osten in Geschichte und Gegenwart* (1951).
† From the official statistics in the *Annuario Pontificio* for 1960.

For every 1,000 Latin rite Catholics, there are twenty-three non-Latin Catholics. One million Eastern Catholics (Syrians, Chaldeans, Armenians, Maronites, and Melkites) live in the U.S.A.

THE EASTERN CATHOLIC LITURGIES

I. THE COPTIC LITURGY

HISTORY

The Copts are the natives of Egypt, the descendants of the ancient Egyptians, whose name was abbreviated by the Arabs to the form *Gupt,* from which is derived the word *Copt.*

They were originally Christians of the Patriarchate of Alexandria, and celebrated the Alexandrian liturgy of St. Mark in Greek. With the rise, however, of the monophysite heresy of Eutyches, an Archimandrite of Constantinople, and the opposition of the monophysite-minded Patriarch Dioscuros of Alexandria to the decisions of the Council of Chalcedon, which in the year 451 condemned that heresy with its teaching of one nature only in Christ (Greek "monos" one, only, and "physis" nature), the majority of the Egyptian Church fell away from Catholicism.

Monophysitism refuses to admit two natures in Christ because it maintains that the human nature was taken up by the divine in the union of the one person. This heresy arose out of opposition to Nestorianism, which taught that in Christ there were not merely two natures, but two persons; but it went too far, and refused to admit the infallible decision of the Church in the matter.

The greater part of the Egyptian people fell into Monophysitism and remains monophysite to this day—the national Church of the Egyptian Christians in that stronghold of Islam.

The head of the Coptic Church is the Patriarch of Alexandria, who elects his own synod of four bishops, and resides in Cairo. His Patriarchate has twenty bishoprics with 900,000 faithful and eight monasteries with about 300 monks.

In the fourteenth and fifteenth centuries attempts were made to win back the Copts to the Catholic Church, but without notable or lasting success. In the seventeenth century the Franciscans succeeded in bringing small groups of Copts back to Catholicism. In 1739 the Coptic Bishop Athanasius of Jerusalem, who resided in Cairo, became a Catholic, and was appointed Vicar Apostolic for the Coptic Catholic community of some 2,000 souls. It was not until the nineteenth century that the number of Coptic Catholics increased to any important extent, and Leo XIII in 1895 erected two dioceses (Minya and Thebes) and the Coptic Catholic Patriarchate of Alexandria (with residence in Cairo), the first Patriarch being Bishop Cyril Macarius. In the past twenty-five years the number of Coptic Catholics has more than doubled to about 80,000; meantime a third diocese has been erected, that of Assiut.

STRUCTURE OF THE MASS

Before the ceremony the priest spreads on the altar a Coptic corporal, and puts on it the chalice, the paten with the host, and five veils: in the center is the chalice, with the paten in front of it on one veil, and two veils on each side.

After vesting, the priest enters the church with the server and bows to the ground before the Holy Doors. In front of the altar he blesses himself and the people with the Coptic hand cross, says the preparatory prayers, and washes his hands. Then comes the Offertory of the host. At a more solemn celebration he uses the prescribed Coptic host. The host is then wrapped in one of the veils and solemnly carried round the altar along with the wine. The Holy Gifts are blessed. After the Offertory follow a prayer of thanksgiving and the epiclesis of God the Son (a prayer for the consecration).

The priest pronounces the *Confiteor* and the absolution before the iconostasis. The server reads the Epistle in Arabic; then follows the Trisagion, the reading of the Gospel by the priest, the petitions, the Creed and the washing of hands.

The Canon begins with prayers for peace. At the *Sursum Corda* and at the *Sanctus* the priest imparts the blessing, with cross and veil, to the people, toward the South, and to himself; and at the *Sanctus* in reverse order.

The climax of the Mass is formed by the consecration, anamnesis and epiclesis of the Holy Ghost. After the diptycha petitions, the priest, while indicating with his left hand the Holy Gifts, imparts a blessing to the people.

Then follow solemn prayers, during which the priest holds his arms outstretched with veils on his hands, the prayer of the fraction, and the first tincture of the Host with the precious Blood, which the priest performs by dipping his finger in the chalice and signing the Host with it.

Now follow the fraction and the Our Father, the prayer of the "Laying-on of Hands," and the absolution prayer to God the Father. The priest next elevates the central particle of the Host, dips it into the chalice, and with it signs the other particles. Then follows the placing of the particle in the chalice.

After a second elevation of the consecrated elements follow a Communion prayer and the Communion of priest and faithful, the thanksgiving, the blessing prayer, and the dismissal blessing.

PARTICULAR POINTS

1. Coptic churches and sanctuaries are bare and simple. The iconostasis is in the form of a wooden partition with three doors, with small square windows between them. Over the central door are icons of the Last Supper and of the twelve apostles, six on each side, with the Archangel Michael and our Lady in the middle. In the sanctuary is a Coptic cross without the figure of

Christ. The Blessed Sacrament is reserved in a side tabernacle. The altar is square and covered with cloth. On it are two to four candlesticks and at times a cross. A chest in the form of a tabernacle, with decorated sides and a circular opening in the top, serves, in ancient churches, as a "throne" for the chalice.

2. The Copts use a corporal made of vestment material.

3. They have as host a loaf of leavened bread about 10 cm. in diameter and 2 cm. high, which is divided into the central square (Despotikon = dominical portion) and twelve other portions. The stamp imprinted on the center of the loaf has for this reason thirteen crosses. For everyday purposes, however, the Catholic Copts use a host of Roman form, but leavened, which they break either into thirteen parts or at first into five only (the other eight being broken off afterwards according to necessity) or, Roman fashion, into three only. A quantity of small hosts for the Communion of the faithful is placed along with the main host on the broad paten.

4. For most prayers, and for blessings, the priest holds a cross in his right hand.

5. For five prayers of the Eucharistic liturgy the priest holds on his extended hands little veils, as a sign of his state of grace, of purity before God.

6. After the Offertory of the host at the beginning of the Mass, the priest wraps it in a veil, shows it to the people, and carries it once round the altar accompanied by the server, who holds the wine. The bread and the wine are blessed on the Gospel side.

7. There is no dismissal of the catechumens.

8. The Copts attach a notable importance to the use of several veils and of the long and broad chalice veil. They inculcate reverence and purity of the soul.

9. Before the Preface, the priest, with cross and veil, blesses the people, then the tabernacle (on the right), then himself; and thereafter he repeats the same blessings in reverse order. The Preface has a double conclusion, for which the priest has the veil upon his hands.

10. On weekdays the epiclesis of the Holy Ghost is said kneeling.

11. After the diptycha the priest points to the paten with his left hand ("Ostension"), and imparts the blessing of the Holy Gifts to the people with cross and veil.

12. The Host is moistened with the precious Blood before the fraction by a finger dipped into the chalice; and after the fraction the remaining particles are touched with the Despotikon dipped into the chalice.

13. Before communicating the priest kisses the host.

14. Before and after distributing Communion, the priest blesses the people with the Holy Gifts saying "Holy Things for the Holy." The particles of the Host are dipped into the chalice at the distribution of Communion.

15. The prayer after the Offertory and thanksgiving is an epiclesis, that is, a prayer for the consecration, addressed to God the Son.

16. There are two prayers of absolution: (a) to God the Son (similar to the *Confiteor* with its absolution); (b) to God the Father before the dipping of the Despotikon in the precious Blood.
17. The Mass begins with a Lord's Prayer, and is closed by a final Our Father and a second last blessing.
18. Apart from the consecration, everything is in Arabic. Sometimes various prayers, for the most part those whose text is familiar, are said in Coptic; the Trisagion and "Peace be to all" are said in Greek.

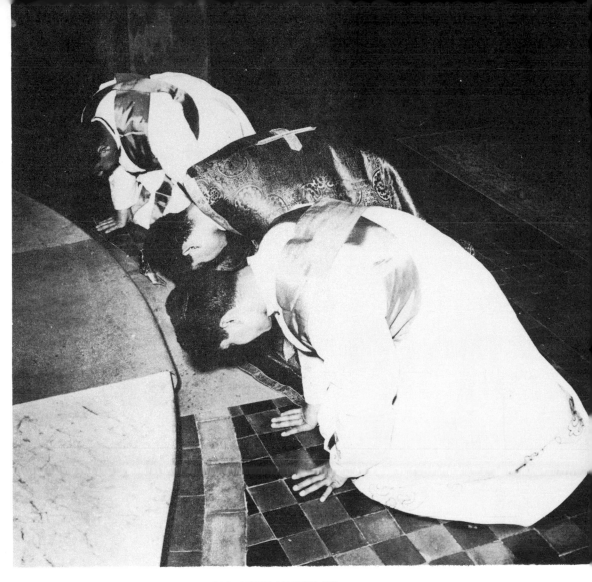

PRAYER OF ADORATION UPON APPEARING IN THE SIGHT OF GOD

"We adore Thee, O Christ, with Thy Father, the Good God, and the Holy Ghost, for that Thou hast come and hast redeemed us.

"Have mercy on us, O Father Almighty, O Most Holy Trinity, O Lord, Strong God, be with us; we have no other stay in our trial, but only Thee.—Make us worthy to say with thanksgiving: Our Father. . . ."

OFFERTORY OF THE BREAD

After a preparatory prayer the priest washes his hands, puts the host upon them, and elevates it: "Grant, O Lord, that our offering be pleasing in Thy sight; deign to accept it as expiation for my sins and the ignorance of this people, that they be sanctified in the gifts of the Holy Ghost. In Christ Jesus, our Lord, through whom are due to Thee honor, glory, praise, and adoration, now and always in all eternity, Amen."

THE VEILING OF THE HOST

"Honor and glory, glory and honor be to the Most Holy Trinity, Father, Son, and Holy Ghost.

"Peace and mercy to the one, sole, holy, catholic, and apostolic Church of God."

PROCESSION WITH THE OFFERINGS

The priest shows the faithful the veiled host, and passes once round the altar with the servers, who carry a lighted candle and the wine.

"Remember, O Lord, those who have brought to Thee these gifts, and those on whose behalf they are offered. Give them in return the heavenly reward."

SHOWING OF SACRED SPECIES (OSTENSIO) AND BLESSING

"O Lord, save Thy people and bless Thine inheritance; feed Thy flock and glorify it for ever. May this blessing, God's power and grace, be with us for ever. Amen."

Still pointing with his left hand to the sacred species, the priest looks toward the faithful and blesses them.

*TINCTURE OF THE SACRED HOST WITH
THE PRECIOUS BLOOD*

The priest—like John the Baptist—points to the Lamb of God, and then dips his
finger in the precious Blood, makes the sign of the cross on both sides of the Host,
saying: "The Holy Body—the precious Blood—Christ, the Lord Almighty—our
God. Amen."

Here all kneel and say: "We adore Thy Holy Body and Thy precious Blood;
Lord, have mercy on us." Then follow the fraction and the Our Father.

12

"SANCTA SANCTIS"

With the words, "Holy Things for the Holy," the priest, bowing his head, elevates the central portion of the sacred Host (Despotikon), dips this slightly into the precious Blood, and with it touches twelve times the other particles (the twelve apostles). "Praised be the Lord Jesus Christ, who hath sanctified these gifts through His Holy Spirit. Amen."

Then the priest takes up the paten along with the veil on which it stands and elevates them with a threefold act of praise of the Blessed Sacrament and faith in the Real Presence: "Amen, amen, amen; I believe, I believe, I believe. . . ."

ACT OF LOVING WORSHIP

Before consuming the sacred Host, the priest says: "Honor unto Thee, Thou Good God, with Thy Father and the Holy Ghost for ever. Amen." Then he kisses it in love and thanksgiving.

After the Communion of priest and people, the Mass comes to an end with a thanksgiving and the blessing prayer.

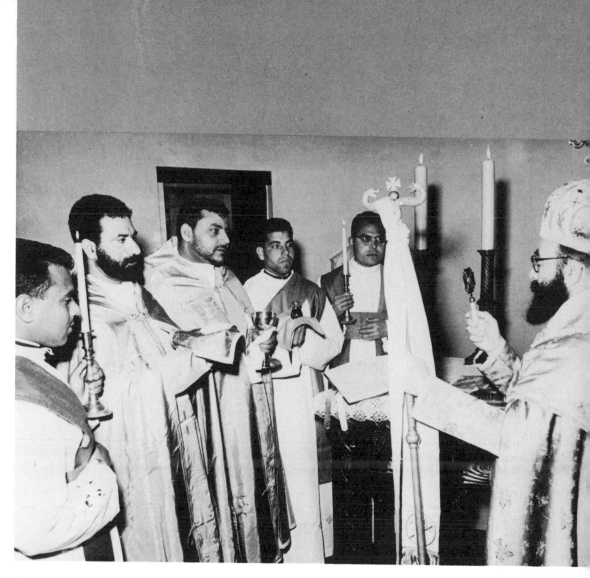

*COPTIC PONTIFICAL—BLESSING OF BREAD AND WINE
AFTER PROCESSION AROUND ALTAR*

"Praised be the Lord, God Almighty. Amen.

"Praised be His only begotten Son, Jesus Christ, our Lord. Amen.

"Praised be the Holy Ghost, the Comforter. Amen.

"Amen, amen, amen. One is the Holy Father, one is the Holy Son, one is the Holy Ghost. Praised be the Lord God for all eternity. Amen.

"All ye nations, praise the Lord; praise Him, all ye peoples. For His mercy is strong upon us, and the Truth of the Lord endureth for ever. Amen. Alleluia."

II. THE ETHIOPIC LITURGY

HISTORY

Several peoples and religions are represented in Ethiopia, the mountainous region running down to the sea to the south of the Sudan. Along the seaboard dwell about six million Mohammedans (about half the total population), and in the western border regions, pagan or superficially Christianized Negro tribes. The nucleus of the Ethiopian Empire is composed, however, of the Semitic people after whom the land is named. These are the four million or so Christian Ethiopians, whose ancestors migrated into Africa, probably from Southern Arabia. Their religious centers are the original capital, Aksum, and Gondar.

The Ethiopian Church was founded from Alexandria. Earliest reliable information goes back only to the middle of the fourth century. St. Athanasius consecrated Frumentius as Bishop of Aksum, at that time the capital of Ethiopia. The metropolitan of Aksum had under his rule six diocesan bishops. These bishoprics, however, were short-lived, since the Patriarchs of Alexandria in later times were unwilling to let an independent Ethiopian hierarchy come into being, and were in the habit of consecrating only one bishop as Abuna ("Father") of Aksum. In this manner the Ethiopian Church was completely attached to Alexandria, and maintained the closest relations with that city. When in the middle of the fifth century the Alexandrian Church fell for the most part into Monophysitism (teaching the unity of nature in Christ) and formed the Coptic Church, it drew Ethiopia, too, into the same error.

After the Arabian invasion Ethiopia was cut off from the rest of the world and left entirely to her own resources. From the seventh to the twelfth century no news of it reached the outer world.

In modern times Alexandria has given the Ethiopian Church several bishops in addition to the Abuna. The *de facto* head of the national Church is the Negus, who has the last word in all important decisions (he is himself a Deacon). The highest ecclesiastical dignitary, the Abuna, has been since 1941 at the same time Abbot General of the monasteries. In addition to the Abuna there are thirteen monophysite bishops in Ethiopia, and one in the Ethiopian monastery in Jerusalem.

There is today a movement in the Ethiopian Church aiming at freedom from the tutelage of the Coptic Church.

RETURN TO THE CATHOLIC CHURCH

While colonizing the seaboard in the seventeenth century, the Portuguese sought to secure an influence over Ethiopia's ecclesiastical relations. The Catholic missionaries, who were so unwise as to seek to Latinize the Ethiopic liturgy, made themselves an object of detestation to the monophysite population. The impetuosity of the Negus, turned Catholic, led to a five-year rising of the Monophysites; and his son expelled all Catholic priests from the country. For over two centuries no Catholic missionary could set foot on Ethiopian soil.

It was not until the nineteenth century that missionary work could be begun in the pagan districts, under the auspices of the Latin rite, by Lazarists, Capuchins, and Cistercians. The missionaries received support from the Italian invaders; unfortunately, after the late war, Catholic missions suffered a severe setback when the missionaries, first the non-Italian, then the Italian ones, were expelled. The Negus, however, has prudently refrained from expelling the Italian immigrants or putting difficulties in the way of their religious practice.

In Asmara, capital of Eritrea, there is a Catholic center. Two native bishops of the Ethiopic rite have been appointed for those Catholic Ethiopians who wish to retain their own ancient rite. There are now 160 Ethiopic Catholic and 20 Roman Catholic, that is, Latin priests, working in Ethiopia; there is an Ethiopic Catholic Cistercian Abbey; there are Capuchins of the Ethiopic rite, Italian teaching Brothers, Lazarist primary and secondary schools; and, working in schools and orphanages, sixty Italian and forty Ethiopic Catholic nuns. The largest Catholic populations are in the Kaffa district in the south, and in Addis Ababa. In the central Galla district there have been established flourishing mission stations. Unfortunately there are not enough Ethiopic Catholic priests; to remedy this lack, Pius XI founded an Ethiopian College in the Vatican State.

STRUCTURE OF THE MASS

After a deep bow the priest goes to the altar, prepares the chalice, and sets the host down before him in the folded veil. After the Prayer of St. Gregory and the Introit prayer, the priest makes a deep reverence and says the prayers at the altar steps.

The Mass begins with the Offertory of the host and of the wine. The Mass of the Catechumens includes a hymn of praise to God who alone is holy, a solemn prayer of praise to the Holy Trinity, and the first "Eucharistic prayer."

After an anticipated litany of petition, the Holy Gifts are covered. There follow a second prayer of praise to the Holy Trinity, the praises of our Lady, and the Epistle, read by the server.

After the Epistle follow the prayers preparatory to the Gospel, along with a blessing imparted to the world. The priest reads the Gospel on the Gospel side, but never turns toward the people to do so, since this is the proper function of the Deacon. After reading the Gospel, he salutes the book by raising it to his forehead. Then comes the dismissal of the catechumens.

In the Mass of the Faithful the priest once more pronounces a solemn Introit prayer, prayers for Church and State and for the faithful present, and finally, the Creed. The Canon is characterized by beginning with the Gloria, to which are attached the prayer for peace and the kiss of peace. Commemoration of our Lord and our Lady, Preface, and *Sanctus* immediately precede the Consecration.

The priest pronounces the formula of institution over the host and lays the latter once more on the paten and makes a deep reverence; then he pronounces the formula over the chalice; then follow the anamnesis and epiclesis (invocation of the Holy Ghost).

The Communion is preceded by the fraction and the Our Father, the prayer of the Laying on of Hands and that of absolution, and the petitions for the living and the dead. There follow a double elevation of the sacred Host, its moistening with the precious Blood, and the placing of a particle in the chalice. Next come the Communion of the celebrant and the distribution of Communion to the faithful, at which the Host is dipped into the precious Blood. The Mass ends with the thanksgiving and the dismissal blessing.

PARTICULAR POINTS

1. The host is lifted up with the veil. The Offertory of bread and wine takes place at the beginning of the Mass.
2. Several prayers and actions point to Syrian influence, for example, the prayer to God as the One Holy One, the blessing to the four quarters of the world, the tilting of the chalice at the Consecration, the moistening with the precious Blood.
3. The Epistle is preceded by the praise of our Lady and followed by a hymn to her.
4. The Trisagion is here addressed to Christ as Man.
5. The moistening of the Host with the precious Blood is accompanied by repeated acts of faith in the real presence of Christ's Body and Blood.
6. The two successive elevations of the sacred Host are accompanied, the first by the *Sancta Sanctis,* the second by forty-one invocations—"Christ have mercy on us," pronounced in alternation by priest and server.
7. On great feast days the Ethiopians use a special Ethiopic host, about 20 cm. wide and a fingerbreadth in thickness, with a corresponding paten. The host is divided into thirteen portions, and the central or "dominical" particle is dipped into the chalice to moisten the others. At Communion the faithful are

given first a particle of the consecrated Host and then a little of the precious Blood, with a spoon. A feast day celebration lasts up to four hours. After the ceremony, and during processions, the choir is accompanied by the rhythm of rattles and drums in a manner which is strange to us, but entirely appropriate.

8. The Ethiopians sign themselves with the back of the thumb, with closed fist. At the mentioning of the Holy Gifts they gesture always with both hands toward paten and chalice: a gesture which is for them a most solemn expression of awe and of faith in the real presence of Christ. In no other rite is this faith so outstandingly expressed.

9. The liturgical language is Geez or Old Ethiopian as spoken and written.

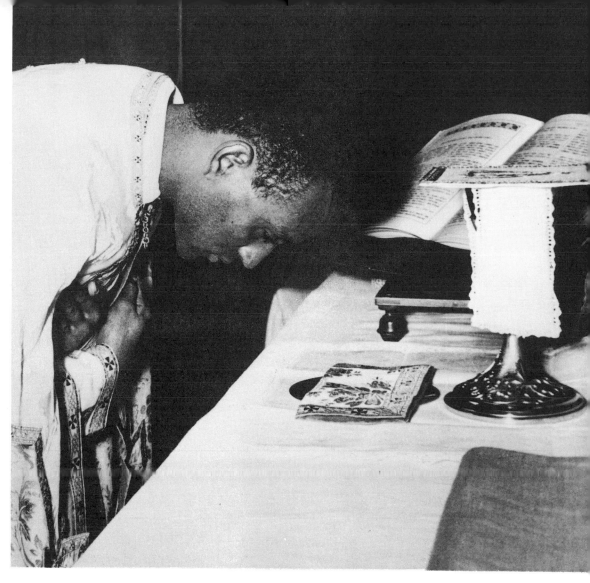

ENTRANCE PRAYER

"O Lord Our God, who in Thy exceeding great love to us men, didst send Thine only begotten Son, to the end that He might lead back the scattered flock, we beg Thee, O Our Master, cast us not out, when we do call upon Thee in this unblemished and dreadful mystery. Not upon our own righteousness do we set our trust, but upon Thy compassion, wherewith Thou hast loved us race of men. We beg and entreat Thee of Thy goodness, O Lover of Mankind, let not this mystery which Thou hast appointed unto our salvation be unto us, Thy servants and Thy whole people, unto condemnation, but unto our salvation, unto the forgiveness of our guilt and of our sins. Honor and glory be unto Thy Holy Name, O Father, Son, and Holy Ghost, now and forever and unto all eternity."

OFFERING OF THE BREAD

The priest lifts the veil with the host upon it, saying: "Lord, Our God, Thou didst graciously accept the offering of Abel in the wilderness, of Noah in the Ark, of Abraham upon the mountaintop, of Elijah upon the Mount of Carmel, and of David upon the threshing floor of the Jebusites, and likewise the widow's mite in the temple. Do Thou likewise accept the sacrifice of Thy servant to the honor of Thy Name, as atonement for my sins and those of the whole people; and be gracious unto us in this world and in the world to come, now and forever and unto all eternity."

22

THE FIRST EUCHARISTIC PRAYER

"O My Lord and Master, Copartner of the Godhead from the beginning, Thou Word of the Father, of one being with Him and the Holy Ghost, Thou art the Bread of Life that camest down from heaven and gavest Thyself, the spotless Lamb, for the Life of the World. We beg and entreat Thee at this time, O Lover of Mankind, by Thy loving kindness and compassion, look graciously down upon this host (points with hands to host) and upon this chalice; and bless this host and sanctify this chalice and purify them both; bless them and change this host into Thy Most Pure Body and that which is in the chalice into Thy precious Blood. May it be for us all comfort, medicine, and healing of our soul, our body, and our mind. For Thou art the King of us all, Christ our God; and to Thee belongeth praise, honor, and worship, together with Thy gracious heavenly Father and the Holy Ghost, the Giver of Life, consubstantial with Thee, now and forever and unto all eternity."

EPISTLE

Before and after the Epistle are sung the praises of the Mother of God. The server reads to the faithful from the Epistle of St. Paul, in the Geez language.

VENERATION OF THE GOSPEL BOOK

The priest prays the Trisagion, the prayer of the Gospel, and gives the blessing to the world. Then he reads, facing the altar, the Gospel of the day. After the reading, he kisses the open book and touches it with his forehead in fervent thanks and veneration.

Then begins the Mass of the Faithful with an Introit, a prayer, and the Creed.

CONSECRATION OF THE WINE

After the priest has consecrated the bread and adored the consecrated Host, he bows over the chalice to pronounce the words of consecration: "Take and drink, this is My Blood, which is shed for you for the salvation of many."

He inclines the chalice in four directions.

VENERATION OF THE SACRED SPECIES

After the Consecration, the priest prays to the Lord, present on the altar. Then
follows the commemoration of the Lord (anamnesis) and the invocation of the
Holy Ghost (epiclesis): "We beg Thee, O Lord, and beseech Thee that Thou
send down Thy Holy Ghost upon this bread and this chalice, that He may change
it into the Body and Blood of our Lord and Saviour Jesus Christ, forever."

27

DISTRIBUTION OF HOLY COMMUNION

The priest dips the Sacred Host into the precious Blood and gives it to the communicants, who stand to receive it, with the words: "This is the Bread of Life which has come down from heaven, the precious Body of Emmanuel, who is verily our God."

The server answers: "Amen. Verily this I do believe."

Thereupon the priest prays in thanksgiving: "And now it is accomplished, Lord, Thy Holy, Unconsumed Mystery, which Thou hast given us unto strength and salvation, in memory of Thy death. We have seen the Mystery of Thy Holy Resurrection. Grant unto us life and maintain us therein, at this time and forevermore. For Thou art a King most Glorious, our Lord and Sovereign, our Saviour, Jesus Christ our God. To Thee do we offer and send up thanksgiving, glory, and honor, together with Thy Heavenly Father and the Holy Ghost, the Giver of Life, from eternity to eternity."

PROCESSION AROUND THE ALTAR WITH CROSS AND PYX

"O Christ, in truth our God, bless us with Thy right hand ✠, bless us with Thy hand ✠, make holy with Thy power ✠, and make strong with Thy Holy Ghost. May this Host avail Thy people unto the remission of sins. Amen.

"I have sought Thy countenance, O Lord; after Thy countenance shall I long again. Turn not away from me Thy countenance, turn not away from Thy servant in Thy wrath. Be Thou my helper; abandon me not and cast me not away, my God and my Saviour.

"O Jesus Christ, High Priest, as Joseph and Nicodemus did wrap Thee in spices and fine linen, wherewith Thou wast well pleased, so mayst Thou also be well pleased in me, Thy servant. Acceptable sacrifice, thanksgiving, and glory be to God the Father unto the remission of sins. Amen."

III. THE SYRIAN LITURGY

HISTORY

The Syrians, in the ecclesiastical sense, are the descendants of the Aramaic Christians of ancient Syria, who have retained the early Christian Syrian rite of Antioch, and who live today chiefly in Iraq. There are Christians of the Syrian rite also in Syria, Lebanon, Egypt, and the United States.

The burgeoning Christian culture in the provinces of the Eastern Roman Empire, above all in Syria, brought the native population a strong cultural and national spirit and consciousness, which strove toward independence from Constantinople.

When the Council of Chalcedon (451) condemned the heresy of the one nature in Christ, the result was violent religious and even political opposition, all the more since the concepts "nature" and "person" had not yet been exactly defined.

Monophysitism quickly spread in Syria, especially in the country districts; indeed, the Monophysites succeeded in placing their candidates on the patriarchal throne of Antioch.

The vacillation of the Greek Emperors, who wanted to placate the Syrians, brought about a state of affairs in which, for seventy years, now Catholic, now monophysite Patriarchs ruled the Church of Syria, in Antioch.

Emperor Justin I (518-527) decided that it was time to settle matters. He suppressed the separatist movements and proceeded most sternly against the Monophysites. His nephew, Justinian (527-555), would have succeeded in overcoming Monophysitism once and for all, had not the Empress Theodora intervened perfidiously in favor of Monophysitism. With the help of the Empress, the monk Jacob Baradai managed to be consecrated bishop. He hurried secretly, disguised as a beggar, through Asia Minor, Syria, and Egypt, and reestablished the Monophysite hierarchy. From then on the monophysite Syrians called themselves "Jacobites," after their organizer. Only in Palestine did the Jacobites fail to gain a firm foothold, thanks to the resistance offered by the Monastery of St. Saba, near Jerusalem.

Thus there were two Churches in Syria: the Catholic minority of the Melkites (the orthodox of the Antioch Patriarchate) and the monophysite Church of the Jacobites.

Since the Jacobites considered the Eastern Romans a hated foreign power, they greeted the Arab conquerors of 636 with open arms. Later they had much to suffer under the Moslems. Many Syrians fell away from Christianity and embraced Islam.

The Dominican and Franciscan missions at the time of the Crusades and during the sixteenth century met with little success. The formation of a Catholic Syrian Church was accomplished only at the beginning of the seventeenth century, when, by the labors of the Capuchins and Jesuits, many Jacobites were won over in Aleppo, among them several bishops and a Patriarch.

A persecution by the Jacobites, lasting nearly 100 years, almost wiped out the Catholic Syrian Church. Toward the end of the persecution (1783), Michael Garveh was elected Patriarch by four Catholic Syrian bishops. He founded a permanent Patriarchate in exile at Charfet, in Lebanon. Patriarch Ephraim II (1898-1929) transferred the Patriarchal See to Beirut.

The Patriarch has under him, besides the Patriarchal diocese, six Archbishoprics, two Bishoprics, two Patriarchal Vicariates, and two Procurators (Rome and Paris). The Catholic Syrians number at present 87,000. Of the 70,000 Jacobites, over 4,000 have been converted in the past twenty years, among them an archbishop.

STRUCTURE OF THE MASS

In his wide-sleeved black cassock, the priest prays the first preparatory prayer before the altar, commends himself to the prayers of the congregation, and kisses the middle of the altar and its edges. With the host in the palm of his hand, he accomplishes the Pre-Offertory. After the second preparatory prayer, he vests and returns to the altar for the third preparatory prayer. Then he raises paten and chalice, holding them in his crossed hands, and says the Second Offertory Prayer, containing a memento of our Lord, our Lady, and the saints, as well as of the faithful departed. Thereupon follows a hymn of praise to the Most Holy Trinity, accompanied by the incensing of the altar, the Gifts, and the people. The priest blesses the Gifts twice, himself once, meanwhile saying the Trisagion (Thrice-Holy). He repeats this action three times. Thereafter the Epistle is read by the server and the Gospel by the priest, who, before and after the reading, blesses the people with the book and says: "Peace be with ye all."

A solemn prayer of entry introduces the Mass of the Faithful. The most stirring glorification of the infinitely Holy Trinity now takes place at the foot of the altar, with the blessing of the chains of the thurible. Then follow the Creed, incensing, and washing of the hands.

The Prayer of Peace and the Kiss of Peace are followed by the Prayer of the Laying on of Hands. After the uncovering of the Holy Gifts, at the Prayer of the Veil, the Pauline blessing is given. After the *Sursum Corda* and *Gratias Agamus* comes the Preface. The Consecration is accompanied, in each case, by a deep bow. There is no elevation of the Sacred Species nor is there any genuflection. After the Memento of the Lord and the Invocation of the Holy Ghost comes the sixfold intercession (Diptycha).

Thereafter there is the threefold breaking of the Bread and the sixfold intinction with the precious Blood. The Admixture of the Sacred Species and the Salutation of Peace are followed by the sixfold blessing, thrice turned toward the altar, thrice turned toward the people. The Our Father is the Prayer of the Sacrificial Banquet. After the Prayer of the Laying on of Hands, the priest elevates the Sacred Species: first the paten, saying: *Sancta Sanctis* (the priest adores the Most Precious Body by touching it to his eyes and lips); then the chalice, saying: *Gloria Patri* (the priest adores the precious Blood in the same manner); then of both species at once, as at the Second Offertory: "Thou only art holy, God the Father . . ." After himself communicating and administering Communion to the faithful, the priest again imparts the sacramental blessing. Then follow thanksgiving and blessing. The priest makes his Postcommunion and takes leave of the altar.

PARTICULAR POINTS

1. The Syrian (Antiochene) liturgy originated in Jerusalem and is called the St. James liturgy after the Holy Apostle James the Less, first Bishop of Jerusalem. The liturgical language is Old Syrian, closely related to the Aramaic language of Jesus and the Apostles. Many prayers, above all the readings, are prayed and sung in Arabic, Turkish, or Kurdish, at services of public worship.

2. There are a number of Anaphoras (Canons) which vary according to the Feast and, indeed, at the will of the reader.

3. Even Low Mass is partly sung (e.g., the words of Consecration). The thurible is always used.

4. At the altar are used: paten without foot, asterisk (metal support of two intersecting bars, with four feet, to hold paten veil away from the Bread). Communion spoon (for priest's Communion only); metal covers may be used instead of the asterisk and the palls.

5. The Host is leavened, ½ cm. thick, signed with thirteen crosses.

6. The Hosts for the people's Communion are intincted with the precious Blood during the Mass, or during the distribution. Thus Communion is under both species.

7. Building upon the prototypes of the Old Testament, the Mass of the Catechumens begins with the "Oblation of Melchisedech" (First Offertory), and, after the vesting of the priest, comes the "Burnt Offering of Aaron" (Second Offertory). There is a triple prayer at the foot of the altar.

8. The Cowl (embroidered humeral) was formerly a mitre and is worn by dignitaries.

9. Repeated *Orate fratres,* with inclinations to either side of the altar and then to the faithful.

10. The "Peace be to you all," accompanied by a simple raising of the right hand and the inclination of the head to the right.

11. With raised thurible, the priest invites the faithful to pray together with him the Our Father, and later the Creed. During the Creed, altar and people are incensed.

12. An expressive action is the glorification of the Most Holy Trinity, on the chains of the thurible: the priest grasps the first chain of the thurible, which is presented to him, and blesses it, saying: "Holy is the Holy One, God the Father"; then he takes two other chains (symbolizing the two Natures in Christ), and blesses them: "Holy is the Holy One, God the Son." At the similar praising of the Holy Ghost, he grasps all the chains. This is a very solemn moment for the Orientals.

13. At the Invocation of the Holy Spirit (epiclesis), the priest performs the same circular motion of the hands as at the Preface.

PREPARATION

"He was led as a lamb to the slaughter; and as a sheep before her shearers is dumb, so He opened not His mouth. Lord, in Thy Holy Place hast Thou builded Thyself a dwelling. Yea, with Thine own Hands hast Thou willed to fashion it withal. May the Lord reign forever! Firstborn of the Father, do Thou accept this Firstborn [Aramaic name for the host] from the hands of Thy humble servant."

SECOND PREPARATORY PRAYER

"O, God, peace loving, meek, and benevolent, and friend of man, Thou desirest
mercy and not offerings, and art more pleased with contrite hearts than with burnt
offerings . . . Accept at this time on the altar of Thy Word, the offerings of our
spirit, and make us worthy to present to Thee our souls, a living and acceptable
sacrifice."

VESTING

"Unclothe me, O Lord, of the stained garments which Satan hath put upon me for my evil works, and clothe me in pure garments, meet for the service of Thy Majesty and the honor of Thy Name . . . Clothe me, O Lord, in a garment that cannot be lost, by the power of Thy Holy Spirit; and grant that, by the practice of pious works, I may be made ever acceptable to Thy will, Father, Son, and Holy Ghost, now and forever. Amen."

PRAYER OF PEACE

The sacrifice is introduced by the prayer of peace: "Merciful and Holy God . . . accept and look with favor upon this Unbloody Sacrifice; grant us the gift of Thy Holy Spirit, and make us worthy, with pure and unburdened conscience, to draw near to the Holy of Holies; grant us Thy peace, which Thy Son did give unto His Holy Apostles, to the end that we, after we have exchanged the holy kiss of peace, may do honor unto Thine almighty goodness, Thy Son, and the Holy Ghost, now and forever."

38

PRAYER OF THE VEIL

The priest lifts the chalice veil from the Holy Gifts and moves it, lowering it thrice, before and behind the chalice: "Thou art the Rock that was riven, out of which did spring the twelve fountains, which quenched the thirst of the twelve tribes of Israel. Thou art the stone that was rolled away from the sepulchre of the Lord."

PAULINE BLESSING

"The Grace of our Lord Jesus Christ and the Love of God the Father, and the fellowship of the Holy Ghost be with you all."

With these words, the priest blesses himself, the other ministers of the altar, and the whole world, in three directions.

40

SURSUM CORDA

"Now let us lift up our souls, our minds, and our hearts!"

GRATIAS AGAMUS

"Let us, with holy fear, give thanks unto God." At the words of the Preface: "Before Thee and all about Thee, stand the Cherubim . . . the Seraphim . . ." the priest describes with his hands several circles above the Holy Gifts, to symbolize the presence of the angels.

MEMENTO AND INTERCESSIONS (DIPTYCHA)

"Almighty God, we offer to Thee this ghostly sacrifice of atonement for Thy Catholic Church, for the Bishops, who do therein proclaim openly the Word of Truth, especially for the Holy Father . . . for our Patriarch. . . ."

The priest lays his hands on the Holy Gifts, then touches his hands to his lips and prays for the ecclesiastical authorities and for all human necessities.

PRIEST'S COMMUNION

"By Thy living and life-giving Blood, which was shed upon the cross, may my guilt be pardoned and my sins forgiven, O Jesus, Word of God, who didst come to redeem us and wilt come to raise us from the dead."

The priest takes from the chalice the particle of the Host, which he reverently receives. Then he drinks from the chalice. The faithful likewise receive under both species.

EUCHARISTIC BLESSING

Before and after the distribution of Holy Communion, the priest gives the faithful communicants the sacramental blessing with the Holy Gifts, saying: "The mercies of God Almighty and of our Redeemer, Jesus Christ, descend upon you all, who at this time bear, distribute, or receive the Holy Gifts. Stretch forth, O Lord, Thine unseen Hand and bless these faithful ones. They worship Thee and receive Thy Body and Thy precious Blood, that they may gain remission of their guilt and forgiveness of their sins and that they may be spotless before Thy Face, our Lord and our God, forever and ever. Amen.

"Glory be to Thee, Glory be to Thee, Glory be to Thee, our Lord and our God, forever and ever. Lord Jesus Christ, may Thy Body, which we have received and Thine atoning Blood, which we have drunk, be unto us, not a judgment and condemnation, but a pledge of life and eternal salvation."

The people pray: "The whole universe doth bow down before Thee and worship Thee. Every tongue doth praise Thy Name; for Thou art the resurrection from the dead and the comforting hope of those now held in the slumber of death. We praise Thee, O our God and we present unto Thee our thanksgiving."

45

ON LEAVING THE ALTAR

"Bide in peace, Thou Holy Altar of the Lord! I know not if I shall soon return to Thee. The Lord grant me the grace to see Thee in the company of the first-born that are in heaven, upon which vision do I set all my hopes. . . . Bide in peace, holy Altar, Thou Table of Life, and be a prayer for me to our Lord Jesus Christ, that I cease not to think of thee, now and forever. Amen."

SYRIAN PONTIFICAL

CONCELEBRATION—ELEVATION OF THE CHALICE
AFTER THE LORD'S PRAYER

"Holy things to the holy (*Sancta Sanctis*).

"One is the Holy Father, who is with us, who in His kindness hath redeemed the world. Amen.

"One is the Holy Son, who is with us; He hath redeemed us with His precious passion. Amen.

"One is the living Holy Ghost, who is with us, Maker and Perfecter of all things that are and have been.

"Blessed be the name of the Lord, now and for ever. Amen."

IV. THE MALANKARESE LITURGY

HISTORY

The Catholic Malankarese go back only thirty years. From the Syrian Jacobites of the Malabar Coast (cf. historical note on the Thomas Christians in the Malabarese rite), a group of 35,000, under the leadership of their Archbishop, Mar Ivanios of Trivandrum, broke away in 1930. These came over to the Catholic Church. To distinguish themselves from the Malabarese who had remained Jacobites, they called themselves "Malankarese." They number at present 108,000 faithful and 180 priests, in two dioceses, with an archbishop at their head.

The Malankarese rite is similar to the Jacobite in Malabar and is a variation of the Syrian rite of Antioch, with many divergent and supplementary practices. The permission to retain the Malayalam language for the celebration of Holy Mass was granted the Malankarese by the Holy Father. The people have been accustomed to it for a long time and so are better able to follow Mass in this way, hearing 90% of the priest's prayers in their mother tongue. The remainder of the Mass is prayed or sung in Syrian.

STRUCTURE OF THE MASS

The priest prays the prayers at the foot of the already prepared altar. Then he vests and commends himself to the prayers of the faithful. The Holy Mass begins with the offering of bread and wine, the incensing of the Gifts and the people, whereupon the praise of the Lord Jesus Christ, the so-called Trisagion, follows. Before the people the server reads the Epistle; the priest, the Gospel. After the reading, the priest does reverence to the Gospel.

The Mass of the Faithful consists of a solemn Entry Prayer, with commemoration on the Mystery of the Feast, an anthem of praise to the Most Holy Trinity with an impressive ceremony on the chains of the thurible, and finally the Creed.

The Eucharistic Sacrifice is introduced by the Prayer of Peace, the Kiss of Peace, and the Prayer of the Laying on of Hands. The Holy Gifts are uncovered, fanned by the veil, lowered before and behind them (signifying the earthquake on Calvary). Then follow the Preface, *Sanctus,* and Consecration, with no elevation of the Sacred Species. After the memento of the Lord (anamnesis) and the Invocation of the Holy Ghost (epiclesis) follow long intercessions for the Pope, the Bishop, the living and the faithful departed, and a memento of the Mother of God.

The repeated breaking of the Bread then follows, with the sevenfold intinction of the Host with the precious Blood—a practice peculiar to the Syrian rite. The third portion of the Mass, the Eucharistic Banquet, begins with the Our Father and the Prayer of the Laying on of Hands. Thereafter comes a threefold elevation of the Sacred Species, at first singly, then together, each time accompanied by a doxology. The Communion of the priest is followed by the Sacramental Blessing and Absolution, Dismissal and Final Blessing, distribution of Communion to the faithful, and the Post-Communion of the priest. Thereafter follows the Thanksgiving.

PARTICULAR POINTS

1. The sanctuary is a chapel, enclosed by high walls, with a door. At all times other than those of the Holy Sacrifice, and for certain periods even of it, the curtain of this door is closed.
2. There is no iconostasis nor are there any prie-dieus.
3. Only the bow and reverential inclination occur in this rite. There is no genuflection.
4. The elevation of the Sacred Species does not occur till the beginning of the Eucharistic Banquet.
5. The offering occurs at the very beginning of the Mass, behind the curtain.
6. The altar is completely enveloped, and the special Malankarese corporal is tricolored: white, green, and red.
7. Thrice the priest commends himself to the prayers of the faithful, before each climax of the Mass.
8. The priest proffers four times during Holy Mass the salutation: "Peace be with you all!" and forthwith administers the sixfold blessing (thrice turned toward the altar, and thrice toward the people).
9. At each salutation the priest symbolically draws forth the blessing from the separate Holy Gifts and dispenses it to the people with his open right hand, while his left remains joined to the altar.
10. Another custom of symbolically drawing forth the blessing from the Holy Sacrifice is the signing of the Tablets (Altar Stone), the paten and the chalice, with a small sign of the cross, which is then transferred upon the missal (upon the names of those being prayed for).
11. A third custom is the "dipping of the blessing," i.e., the cupping of the hands over chalice and paten and the laying of the hands thereafter upon the breast (the "Kiss of Peace"). The priest repeats this action six times during the Intercessions.
12. The Malankarese Mass is easily the richest in symbolism of all Oriental liturgies.

PRAYER BEFORE THE ALTAR AFTER PREPARATION

"O Pure and Holy One, who dwellest in the spheres of light, take away from us evil passions and thoughts impure. Help us, with a pure heart, to do the works of justice . . . O Lord, in Thy Holy Place hast Thou built Thyself a dwelling. Lord, do Thou prepare it with Thine own hand. May the Lord reign forever."

Beside the covered chalice, which is placed upon the pendant corporal, an asterisk, Communion spoon, and a small water cruet are needed for the celebration of Holy Mass.

ORATE, FRATRES

"My dearly beloved brethren, pray for me, I beseech you, in the love of the Lord, that Christ may accept my sacrifice."

The eucharistic service of intercession begins with the offering of bread and wine, the incensing of the Gifts and the people, to which latter action is conjoined the praise of the Lord Jesus Christ.

TRISAGION

"Holy God—Holy Strong One—Holy Immortal One, who wast crucified for us, have mercy upon us."

At the first invocation, the priest lays the fingers, with which the blessing is given, on the edges of the altar; at the second, on the paten and altar's edge; at the third, on the chalice, paten, and altar; and then makes the sign of the cross over himself. The acolyte answers each time: "Have mercy upon us!"

VENERATION OF GOSPEL

"For the Gospel of Life, that He hath proclaimed unto us, be honor, praise, and thanks, unto our Lord, Jesus Christ, now, and forever and ever. And to the Father, who hath sent Him for our salvation; and to the Holy Ghost, who hath given us the gift of life."

HYMN OF PRAISE TO THE MOST HOLY TRINITY

Even as the Mass of the Catechumens has its hymn of praise to the Lord Jesus Christ (Trisagion), so also the Mass of the Faithful has its hymn of praise to the One-in-Three (Doxology), symbolized in the three chains of the thurible. The priest grasps one chain, blesses it, and says: "Holy is the Holy One, God the Father"—Amen—Then he grasps two further chains, blesses them, and says: "Holy is the Holy One, God the Son"—Amen—Finally he grasps all three chains, blesses them, and says: "Holy is the Holy One, God the Holy Ghost!"—Amen.

54

KISS OF PEACE

"May Thy peace and Thy rest, O Lord, Thy Love and Thy Grace and the Mercy of Thy Godhead remain with us and among us, all the days of our life." The priest first kisses the altar, then the chain of the thurible. The acolyte touches with his forehead the priest's hand, kisses it, and transmits the kiss of peace to the congregation by handclasp.

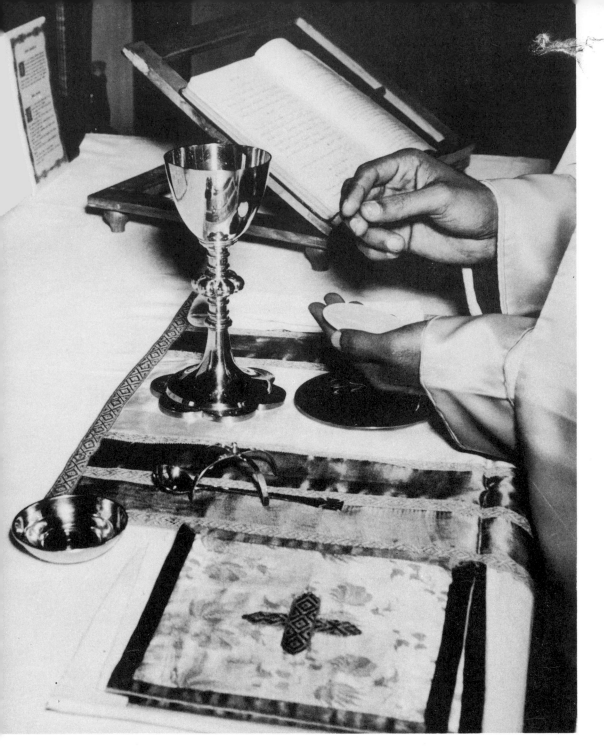

CONSECRATION OF THE HOST

"In the night in which He was delivered up for the life and the redemption of the world, He took bread into His Holy Hands, raised it toward heaven, blessed it, sanctified, broke, and gave it to the Apostles, His Disciples, saying: 'Take and eat; this is My Body which is broken for you and for many for the redemption of sins and unto life everlasting.' "

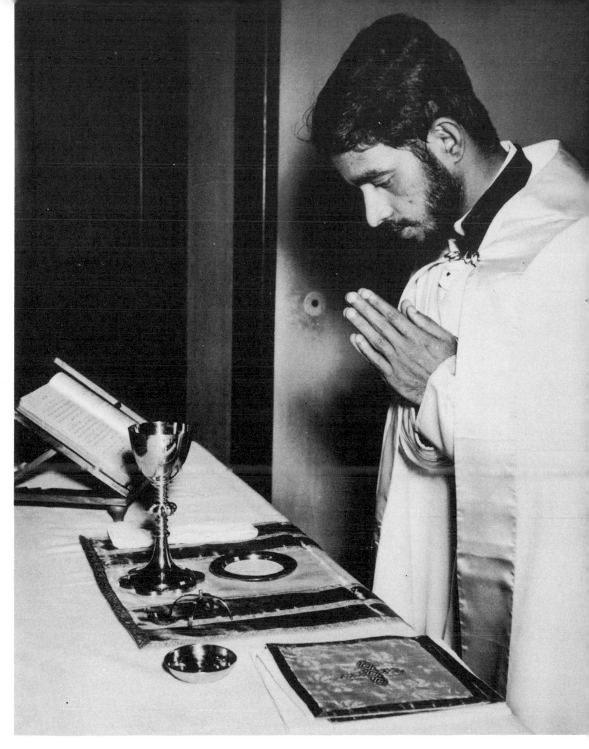

MEMENTO OF THE LIVING (DIPTYCHA)

After the commemoration of the Lord (anamnesis) and the invocation of the Holy Ghost (epiclesis), the priest commemorates all those who are entered in the Diptycha (lists), among them the Holy Father and the Archbishop . . . "that they may rule and lead the people in all purity and holiness." At each memento, the priest "scoops" the blessing with both hands above the chalice and paten, and folds his hands on his breast, in sign of the kiss of peace.

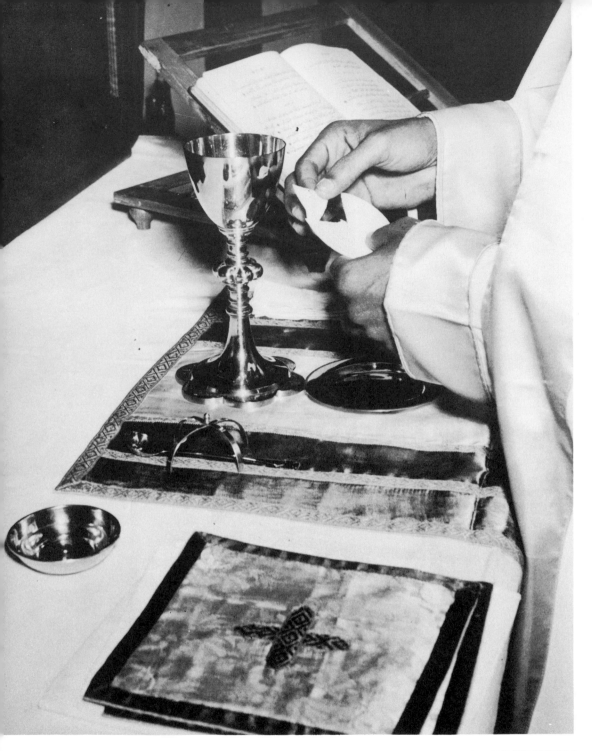

THE INTINCTION

"Behold, O Father, our sins, but behold also this Sacrifice of Thy Son, which hath infinitely more weight than our transgressions . . . because I have sinned, Thy dearly-beloved Son hath suffered so much for me. His sufferings suffice to appease Thee; by them I gain life."

So saying, the priest, with a particle of the Sacred Host which he has dipped into the precious Blood, touches the other particles in remembrance of the precious Blood which Christ shed for us.

THE FINAL BLESSING AFTER HOLY COMMUNION

"Great and wonderful God, Thou hast bowed the heavens and come down to redeem our humanity; look down upon us according to Thy compassion and Thy grace. Bless Thy people and preserve Thine inheritance, that we may always praise Thee. Thou art Our True God, with God the Father who hath begotten Thee, and with the Holy Ghost, now and forever and unto ages of ages. Amen."

BEGINNING OF THE CANON (ANAPHORA)

· "O God, Lord of the Universe, Lover of Man, make us worthy of this service, who are so unworthy, and grant that, being freed from all unrighteousness and acceptance of persons, we may impart peace one to another in a holy and godly embrace, linked by the bond of love and peace; through God our Lord, our Redeemer Jesus Christ, Thine only-begotten Son, through whom and with whom belong to Thee honor and glory and might, with Thine All-Holy Ghost, the Adorable, the Lifegiver, of one nature with Thee, now and forever and unto all ages. Amen.

"O Lord, bless them that bow their heads before Thee . . . God the Father, turn not away from us Thy countenance, as we offer Thee this godly sacrifice. We do this not trusting in our righteousness, but with the hope of Thy mercy. . . ."

V. THE MARONITE LITURGY

HISTORY

The Maronites, like the Syrians and the Melkites, are descendants of Aramaic Christians of ancient Syria. Since about the eighth century, they have lived in the mountains of Lebanon and are all Catholics.

Originally, the Maronites belonged to the party in the Antioch Patriarchate which had remained orthodox. To restore in his kingdom the peace which had been disturbed by the apostasy of the Jacobites and to win over the Monophysites, the Emperor Heraclius tried a compromise by propagating the doctrine of Monotheletism (the one will in Christ). But the result was simply to bring into being a new group, calling themselves "Maronites" after the holy monk, Maron, who had lived at the beginning of the fifth century. Upon his grave a monastery arose, whose monks had fought zealously against Monophysitism, in the sixth century.

The new religious group retained its monotheletic formulas, even after the Council of Constantinople (681) had condemned Monotheletism; but they were never willing to admit that they had separated themselves from the Catholic Church. (This question has often been discussed by specialists, but has never been positively clarified.)

Thus there were, in eighth century Syria, three religious communions: Monophysites (Jacobites), Melkites, and Maronites, each regarding the others as heretics. The Maronites withdrew to the mountains of Lebanon, where they founded a Patriarchate. In the year 1181, at the time of the Crusades, the entire body of the Maronite faithful, together with their bishops and Patriarch, made their peace with Rome.

The 1935 statistics show over 355,000 Maronites. Today there are 533,000. Numerically they are the strongest religious community in Lebanon. On the island of Cyprus there are about 3,000; there are many times that number in Palestine and Egypt, and over 50,000 in the U.S.A.

STRUCTURE OF THE MASS

The priest goes to the altar, genuflects, puts down the chalice, and after bowing in such a way as to form, in three movements, a sign of the cross with his forehead, says the Introductory Prayers, his folded hands resting upon the altar.

Before the offering of the bread and wine, he incenses the various sacred vessels. After the prayers at the foot of the altar occurs the first incensing of the

Gifts, the altar, and the people. After the Kyrie and Trisagion (Thrice Holy) comes the memento, with a memento of our Lord and His Blessed Mother.

Thereupon are said the second Entry Verse and Prayer; then follows the second incensing of Gifts, altar, and people, accompanied by the *Miserere* prayer, prayer of Penance, Anthem of Praise, and prayer for the Church.

At the second Trisagion the priest incenses the Gifts a third time. The server reads the Epistle to the people in Arabic, and the priest reads the Gospel. Before and after the Gospel, the priest imparts the blessing saying: "Peace be with you."

The Mass of the Faithful contains a Eucharistic Hymn, the Creed, with the fourth incensing of Gifts, altar, and people—and finally the washing of the hands.

The Eucharistic Sacrifice and the Canon begin with the Kiss of Peace. Before the *Sursum Corda* the Pauline Blessing is imparted, the priest blessing in three directions with the veil; after the Preface come the *Sanctus* and the holy moment of the Consecration, with anamnesis, and Invocation of the Holy Ghost (epiclesis), and the Diptycha. Then comes the Prayer of the breaking of Bread.

Thereafter the Sacred Species are elevated and finally the Host is elevated alone. The second elevation of the separated Sacred Species takes place after the Blessing of Exorcism, the Our Father and the Prayer of the Laying on of Hands. After this Elevation come the Anthem of Thanksgiving, Breaking of Bread, Intinction of the Host with the precious Blood, and the Commingling of the Sacred Species.

Before communicating, the priest says a Prayer of Preparation and strikes his breast three times. He imparts to the faithful the Blessing of Exorcism and the Blessing of Absolution. After distribution of Holy Communion to the faithful and the Memento of the Faithful Departed, the priest consumes what remains of the Sacred Species, pronounces the Thanksgiving Prayer, gives the Final Blessing, and takes leave of the altar.

PARTICULAR POINTS

1. The Maronites have several Anaphoras (Canons) which vary at the will of the celebrant; the most frequently used is "The Anaphora of the Holy Roman Catholic Church, the Mother of All Churches."
2. The Latin Mass vestments (black in Requiems), the unleavened Latin hosts, the form of distribution of Holy Communion—all show obvious Latin influence.
3. The offering comes first; then the Prayers at the Foot of the Altar.
4. Incensing occurs five times even in Low Mass: before the offering, at the First and Second Entry Prayers, at the Second Trisagion, and at the Creed.
5. The Blessing is frequently pronounced with outstretched arms, the priest blessing the people at the beginning, in the middle, and at the end, with the hand cross from which hangs a silken ribbon.

6. At the Pauline Blessing the priest blesses the Holy Gifts and the servers with the chalice veil.

7. At the end of the Preface and at the epiclesis, the priest circles his hands round both sides of the chalice in an upward movement. This signifies the presence and action of the Holy Ghost or the heavenly hosts.

8. Most expressive is the ceremony of the Kiss of Peace at the beginning of the Canon. The server kneels to the right of the priest and extends his right hand in a gesture of supplication. The priest kisses the chalice veil, touches the altar, the chalice, and the host, and then places his hand in that of the server, to transmit the Peace of the Lord.

9. Notable is the kneeling of the priest at the epiclesis, and the threefold touching by the celebrant with his fingertips of the edge of the altar and of his lips: "Hear me, O Lord."

10. The Sacred Banquet begins with the "Prayer of the Breaking of Bread and the Signing"; the priest breaks the edge of the Sacred Host in four places and makes with it eighteen signs of the Cross over the precious Blood.

11. The Blessing of Absolution with paten or chalice to right or left outside the corporal is another form of the Syrian Blessing of Absolution before the distribution of Holy Communion.

12. The Maronite Communion Hymn of Mar Jacob of Sarouq is prayed in the Mass of the Syrians, Malankarese, and Malabarese, in various forms.

13. The leave-taking of the altar is a characteristic of all Syrian rites.

PRAYER AT BEGINNING

"I will go up unto the altar of God, to God who rejoices my youth. Into Thy house have I entered in, O God, and before Thy throne have I fallen down, O heavenly King. Pardon me all my sins, which I have committed against Thee."

Then the priest mounts the altar steps. He folds his hands and recollects himself in prayer: "Bind the sacrifice with cords, even unto the horns of the altar" (Ps. 118: 27).

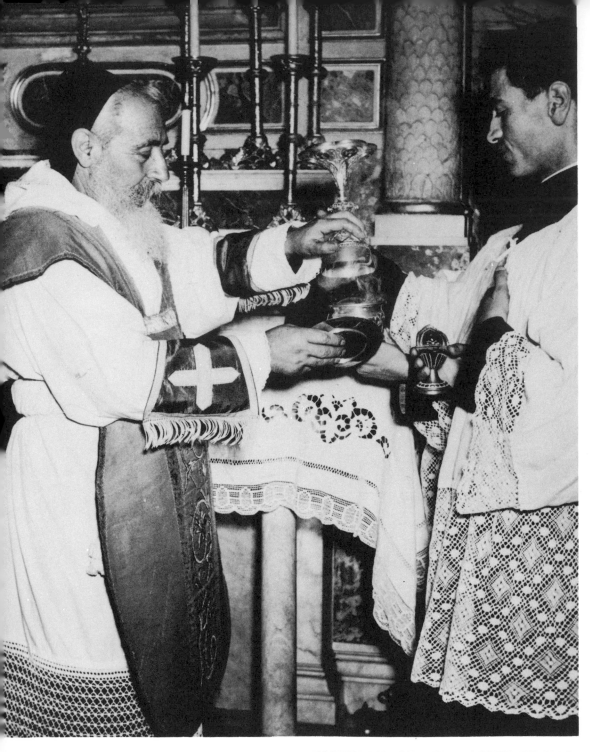

INCENSING OF THE SACRED VESSELS

All the instruments of the altar are incensed. The priest holds chalice and paten inverted over the rising incense clouds. Then he blesses the host and prays: "O great and ever-loving God, Thou hast accepted the vows, the gifts, the first fruits, the tithes of Thy faithful servants: do Thou, now, likewise, accept the gifts here presented by these, Thy servants, which they have chosen and do offer for the love of Thee and to the honor of Thy Holy Name."

MEMENTO

"Before Thee do I spread forth my hands and my heart. Pardon me my transgressions . . . I am not worthy; therefore, do I pray Thee, preserve my soul from
the attacks of the infernal fiend and set a guard before my eyes, against their
lascivious gazing; before my ears, against their vain hearing; before my hands,
against their shameful working; and so keep my heart that it may be but for Thee;
and that I be quite turned in all things to Thee and to Thee alone, to the end that
the gift of Thy Divine Mysteries may be assured unto me."

Then gifts, altar, and people are incensed again.

INCENSING

While the priest envelops altar and Holy Gifts in clouds of incense, he prays the penitential psalm, "Miserere" (Ps. 50).

Then follows the prayer of the *Miserere:* "Have mercy upon us, O God, according to Thy grace; through Thy goodness, pardon our sins; cleanse our unrighteousness by Thy manifold and great mercies. Create in us a pure heart and a humble spirit; sanctify our thoughts, make them purer than burnt offerings. Teach mankind Thy ways; lead the erring ones to Thee again, to the end that their tongues may praise Thy righteousness and earn Thy everlasting mercies, Father, Son, and Holy Ghost."

"PEACE BE UNTO YOU ALL—AND WITH THY SPIRIT."

Between the Epistle, which the server reads to the people in the native Arabic,
and the Gospel, the priest gives the faithful the blessing and the kiss of peace.

KISS OF PEACE

The priest says to the server: "Peace be unto thee, thou servant of the Holy Ghost."

The server kisses the priest's hand and says: "Come in peace, our father and holy priest."

The server transmits the kiss of peace. Giver and receiver clasp hands. The receiver withdraws his hands and places them over his heart.

The Pauline Blessing, the *Sursum Corda,* and the Preface and Sanctus introduce the sacrifice.

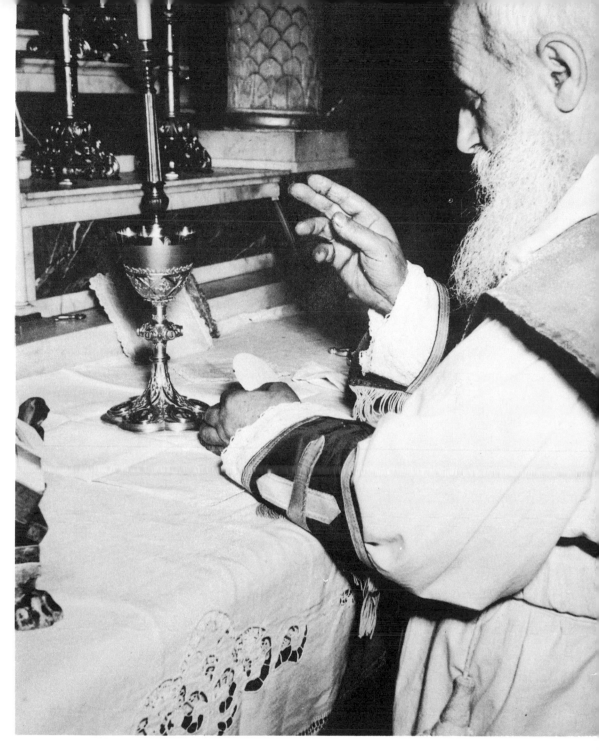

CONSECRATION

The priest blesses the Gifts and speaks the words of consecration over them: "On the day before His suffering, He took bread into His holy Hands, lifted up His eyes unto Thee, O God, His Father Almighty in heaven, gave thanks unto Thee, blessed the bread, sanctified, and broke it and gave it to His disciples, saying: "Take, eat, this is My Body." (These last words are sung.)

COMMUNION PRAYER

"Make us worthy, O Lord and God, that Thy Holy Body may sanctify our bodies and Thy Holy Blood wash our souls; and that this may be unto us pardon of guilt and forgiveness of sins, O Thou, our Lord and God, to Thee be glory forever."

72

POSTCOMMUNION

Before the dismissal of the faithful, the priest consumes what remains of the Sacred Species and prays: "By Thy living and life-giving Blood, may my guilt be remitted and my sins forgiven, O Jesus, Word of God, who hast come for our salvation."

ON LEAVING THE ALTAR

The priest dismisses the congregation with the words: "Dearly beloved brethren, go in peace. We commit you to the grace of God, to the Most Holy Trinity." Then he gives the blessing: "The blessing of our Lord Jesus Christ descend from heaven upon ye and me."

After a long final prayer, the priest takes leave of the altar with the words: "Bide in peace, thou holy Altar. O that I may be vouchsafed to return to thee in peace . . . and, at the time appointed to appear, free of all guilt and not confounded before the judgment seat of Christ. Bide thou in peace. I know not if I shall return even once more to thee, to celebrate the Holy Sacrifice."

MARONITE PONTIFICAL

"We praise and exalt in songs and hymns the Holy Ghost, and bring to mind the all-holy ever-virgin Mother of God, Mary, and take her as our advocate before Her Son, that was born of Her blessed womb, and make this entreaty: 'Through the intercession of Thy blessed Mother, keep, O Lord this land and them that dwell therein from the hard blows and the consequences of Thy wrath. Turn away danger and disturbance, war, devastation, famine, and disease. Have compassion on our lowliness, heal the sick, strengthen the weak among us, and succor the persecuted; and to the faithful departed give eternal rest and make us all worthy of a happy and peaceful end, that we may glorify Thee and Thine ever-blessed Father and Thine ever-living Holy Ghost, until the end of ages.' "

VI. THE GREEK LITURGY

HISTORY

The transfer of the Roman capital to Constantinople (Byzantium) lent a new importance to that city as the ecclesiastical metropolis of the Greek East.

Soon (in 451 A.D.) the Patriarchate of Constantinople was created. The ambition of the Greek people and of its pastors, encouraged by the emperor and the imperial court, sought perpetually to raise Constantinople to the rank of a second ecclesiastical Rome, and to the highest ecclesiastical authority in the Eastern Empire. The Eastern emperors aimed in this manner to extend their authority over the Church as a whole, in addition to their civil supremacy. This ambition found allies in the rivalries, the national conflicts of interests, and the profound divergences in cultural and political institutions, which lay between the peoples of the West and of the East. The result was a growing estrangement of the entire Christian East from the West and from the Roman Papacy. Constantinople attained an ecclesiastical hegemony in the Eastern Empire, while the other Eastern Patriarchates were severely weakened by dogmatic disputes and schisms, and finally by the Arab invasion.

And so it happened that the Greek Patriarchate of Constantinople became powerful and conscious of its own importance and began to set itself up against the Roman Mother Church, from which it became more and more estranged. Finally an open rupture ensued. Political and ecclesiastical disputes over jurisdiction over the Balkans and the Greek possessions in Italy, and misunderstandings founded on differences in liturgical practice, led on both sides to widespread enmity and hatred. Finally, the misunderstandings and mistakes of the political and ecclesiastical leaders of West and East led to the failure of all attempts to reconciliation, and, in the eleventh century, to open schism, which has lasted to our own day.

There had already been a schism of thirty-five years at the turn of the sixth century. In 859 Patriarch Photius of Constantinople began an open war against the Pope and the Roman Church. In 1054, the Patriarch Michael Caerularius brought the whole people into such conflict with the West that opposition and rupture were definite.

An unsuccessful attempt at reconciling the Greek and Latin Churches was made in 1098. The reunion imposed by force on the Greeks by the Latin Empire of Constantinople (1204-1261) did not last.

In the centuries which followed, various Greek emperors sought reunion with Rome, but from purely political motives.

For her part, the Roman Church made yet greater efforts to win back the East.

A union was reached at the Ecumenical Council of Lyons (1274), but it did not last.

The Council of Ferrara-Florence (1439) brought about a union in view of the Turkish menace, but the people were discontented; and hostile forces, especially the other Eastern patriarchates, once more brought to nothing the reunion of Greece and Rome.

Finally a third great attempt at reunion of the Churches succeeded in 1452, when the Turks were at the gates of Constantinople. The capture of the city by the Turks put an end to this union, the people being still hostile.

The Roman invitation to the General Council of the Vatican in 1868 was brusquely declined by Constantinople.

So it is that the Greek Church remains in schism, only a small fraction of it being in union with the Catholic Church.

STRUCTURE OF THE MASS

After the preparatory prayers, the priest vests and goes to the preparation table on the north side of the sanctuary for the preparation of the elements (Proskomidi). After the opening prayer, the Introit, and the first litanies have been said at the altar, he passes round the altar with the Gospel book, comes out of the sanctuary with it, and makes with it the Lesser Entrance through the Royal Doors of the iconostasis. After the Trisagion come the Epistle and Gospel, and other litanies, and the dismissal of the catechumens; then follow the litanies of the Mass of the Faithful, the Hymn of the Cherubim, and the Greater Entrance with chalice and paten, a petition litany, and the Creed.

The anaphora is introduced by the Pauline formula of blessing and the *Sursum Corda*. After the Preface and the *Sanctus* follows the Consecration with the anamnesis, an elevation of the Sacred Species, and the epiclesis. Then follow the commemorations and petitions of the diptychs.

The Communion is preceded by a blessing and a litany of petition, followed by the Our Father and an elevation of the Host. At the fraction the priest puts a particle of the Host in the chalice. The priest receives the Body of Christ and drinks of the chalice. He next communicates the faithful. After taking the chalice to the preparation table and chanting the litany of thanksgiving, he says the prayer of the blessing, gives the dismissal blessing, and distributes blessed bread (antidoron), but only in a solemn Mass.

PARTICULAR POINTS

1. During the earlier part of the Mass and at its end, the priest often wears the headdress called "kalimafkion" up to the Hymn of the Cherubim, and from the Communion on.
2. The Mass vestment is in the form of a cape reaching to the ankles on all sides, of flexible material. During the preparation of the elements the priest so arranges it that it hangs like a stole; at the beginning of the Mass he allows it to hang freely behind him for liturgical action.
3. In bowing down before making the sign of the cross, the priest reaches low down with the right hand, as a symbol of his lowliness before God.
4. The leavened altarbread is about 10 cm. across and 5 cm. thick. A cube is cut from the center of the host to be consecrated; in commemoration of our Lady a triangular pyramidal particle is cut out; for the other commemorations oblong prisms are cut out. Often, however, leavened altar bread in the form of flat squares are used. All the particles are consecrated.
5. The paten is a flat one with a rim, but with no foot.
6. The small chalice veil is in the form of a strip of material which hangs down over two sides of the chalice.
7. At the beginning of the preparation (Proskomidi) the priest holds in his hands the altar bread as well as the lance.
8. The offertory prayer of the preparation is said with hands outstretched.
9. The server turns toward the people to read the Epistle.
10. After the Epistle the reader bows to the ground for the priest's blessing.
11. During the prayer for the catechumens, the priest opens the antimension with a Roman corporal on it.
12. Before the Greater Entrance with chalice and paten, the priest arranges the chalice veil so that it hangs over his back.
13. At the Creed the priest first holds the veil by its upper edge and waves it in front of the chalice, then once around it; then he folds it several times and holds it between the middle fingers of his right hand; at the end of the Creed he waves it, so held, several times with a circular motion around the chalice.
14. The priest begins the Pauline formula of blessing while making the sign of the cross over chalice and paten with the veil (held as above); then he turns to the people and blesses them with the veil.
15. Still holding the veil, he stretches out his hand, at the *Sursum Corda,* turned toward the people; at the *Gratias Agamus* he crosses himself with it and bows to the icon of the Saviour on the iconastasis.
16. At the closing words of the Preface the priest folds the asterisk and with it strikes the edge of the paten four times, in the sign of the cross.
17. At the words "He took bread" before the consecration, the priest raises the paten and holds it in his left hand while blessing it.

18. After the commemoration of our Lady which follows the consecration, the priest takes the dish with the particles of bread left over from the preparation, which are to be distributed as "antidoron" at the end of the Mass, and holds it for a moment over the chalice, then gives it back to the server and blesses it.

19. The priest stretches forth his hands at the *Pater Noster.*

20. At the Prayer of the Laying on of Hands the priest bows down with hands extended under the vestment as an expression of thanksgiving.

21. Communion may be distributed to the faithful with a spoon or, as in the illustration, by taking the oblong particle from the paten, dipping it in the chalice, and administering it thus to the communicant. This is the common practice. The remaining particles are afterwards put into the chalice.

22. The Prayer of the Blessing is said before the icon of the Saviour on the iconostasis. The blessing is given simply with the hand.

23. Before leaving the altar, the priest says a final prayer turned toward the preparation table.

24. The Royal Doors are open:
    a. from the Lesser Entrance until after the Gospel;
    b. from the Greater Entrance until the Litany;
    c. after the Creed until the Preface;
    d. from the Communion of the faithful until after the Last Blessing.

25. The curtain of the Royal Doors is (commonly) drawn shut:
    a. after the Greater Entrance until the beginning of the Creed;
    b. after the *Sanctus* until the beginning of the commemoration of our Lady;
    c. at the beginning of the Litany until the Our Father;
    d. after the Prayer of the Laying on of Hands until the Communion of the faithful.

VESTING

"Thy right arm, O Lord, hath wrought wonders of might. Thy right arm, O Lord, hath smitten Thine enemies to the ground. Before the fulness of Thy magnificence, Thy foes sink into the dust."

BLESSING THE ALTAR WITH THE GOSPEL BOOK

First there is the Proskomidi, i.e., the preparation of the offerings at the prothesis. Then the priest begins the liturgy with the solemn Introductory Prayer: "O heavenly King, the Paraclete, Spirit of Truth, everywhere present and permeating all things, Treasury of blessings and Giver of life, cleanse us from every stain and save our souls, O gracious Lord."

Now the priest takes the Gospel book and makes over the altar a large cross with it saying: "Blessed be the kingdom of the Father, and the Son, and the Holy Ghost, now and always and for ever, world without end."

CREED

"I believe in . . . the Holy Ghost, the Lord and Giver of Life. . . ."

The priest swings the veil during the Creed and waves it once round the chalice to symbolize the Holy Spirit.

SURSUM CORDA

"Lift up your hearts," cries the priest with outstretched arms, turned toward the people. Then he prays the Preface, turned toward the altar: "It is meet and right that we should hymn Thee, laud and praise Thee . . . for Thou art God, the Ineffable, the Unfathomable, the Invisible, the Incomprehensible. In Thee is the fulness of eternal life. . . ."

CONSECRATION

The priest lifts up the host, blesses it, and sets the paten down again. Then he holds his hand in blessing over the paten and pronounces the words of consecration: "Take and eat, this is My Body, which is broken for you for the forgiveness of sins."

Thereafter follows the consecration of the wine.

THE REUNION OF THE SEPARATED SPECIES

"The fulness of the Holy Ghost!"

    With these words, the piece of the consecrated Host, which bears upon it the Name of Jesus, is put into the chalice by the priest.

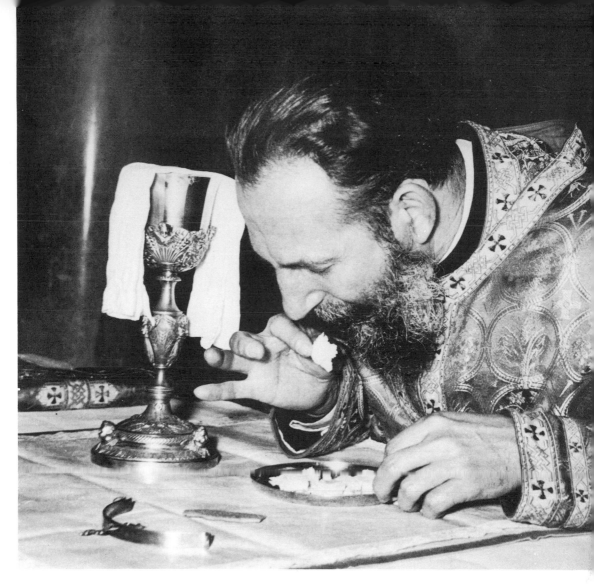

COMMUNION OF THE PRIEST

"Give me, O Lord, the precious and all-holy Body of our Lord and God and Saviour Jesus Christ."

The priest with great reverence consumes the Sacred Host. After Communion he prays: "This has touched my lips and will take away my iniquities and will cleanse my sins."

DISTRIBUTION OF COMMUNION

"I believe, O Lord, and I confess, that Thou art indeed the Christ, the Son of the Living God, who didst come into the world to save sinners, of whom I am the chief. Likewise do I believe that this is truly Thy Most Pure Body and that this is verily Thy precious Blood.

"Make me this day, O Son of God, a sharer in Thy Mystic Supper, for I will not reveal the mystery to Thine enemies, nor will I give Thee a kiss, like unto Judas, but like unto the Good Thief, I will confess Thee: Remember me, O Lord, in Thy kingdom. Grant, O Lord, that the participation in Thy Holy Mysteries may not be for me a cause of judgment and condemnation, but for the healing of my soul and body."

The priest dips particles of the Host in the precious Blood and gives them to the communicants with the words: "The servant of God partakes of the precious and holy Body of our Lord and Saviour Jesus Christ unto the remission of his sins and unto life everlasting."

SOLEMN CONCELEBRATION IN ST. PETER'S.
THE CONSECRATION.

VII. THE MELKITE LITURGY

HISTORY

Syria and Egypt were Roman provinces and were incorporated into the Eastern Roman Empire. Ecclesiastically, however, these countries were subject to Patriarchs of their own in Antioch and Alexandria, and were entirely independent of the Byzantine Patriarch. They had their own ecclesiastical organization and their own liturgies, which they celebrated in Greek and in the local Syriac and Coptic languages.

When the monophysite heresy arose in the fifth century (teaching that there was only one nature in Christ), the Patriarchates of Alexandria and Antioch both fell away, with the exception of a small minority.

Monophysitism had gained the upper hand in these lands, except for the Patriarchate of Jerusalem, and so gave rise to the Jacobite Church in Syria and the Coptic one in Egypt.

Those Christians who remained faithful to orthodoxy were given by the Monophysites the nickname "Melkites," that is, "King's men," on account of their fidelity as Greeks or Grecophiles to the Emperor (in Syriac *malka*). Subsequently the Melkites suffered more severely than the Monophysites from the incursions and persecutions of the Persians, Arabs, and Mongols. Many of them fell away from the Faith under persecution, especially under the persecution of the Mohammedanized Mongols.

In Lebanon, the Maronites formed a quite separate community. Unfortunately, the rest of the Melkites faithful to Byzantium were drawn into the schism of the eleventh century. Thus there are today the three schismatic Patriarchates of Alexandria, Antioch, and Jerusalem. They call themselves, however, not "Melkites," but simply "Orthodox," in keeping with the practice of Eastern Catholics before the schism, who referred to themselves as "Orthodox" in opposition to the Monophysites.

Under the tutelage of Constantinople during the period of Moslem oppression, the Melkites gave up their own original Syrian and Alexandrian liturgies and, in the thirteenth century, took over from Constantinople the Byzantine rite. The Byzantine liturgical books were translated into Syriac, the usual liturgical tongue; but since the seventeenth century, the Melkite Byzantine liturgy has been celebrated in Arabic, with some remnants of Greek.

Catholic missionary activity among the Melkites began in the seventeenth century. Many adherents were won, especially in Aleppo and Damascus. In Egypt, too, Catholic communities were formed among the Syrian Melkite emigrants.

In the year 1701 two bishops returned in secret to Catholic unity. The Catholic Melkites have stood up well under persecution. In Aleppo, as also in southern

Lebanon and in Syria, they have well-organized communities and, in Jerusalem, a seminary of their own, which publishes an excellent periodical.

The Catholic Melkite Patriarch resides at Damascus and bears the title "Patriarch of Antioch, Alexandria, and Jerusalem, and of all the East." Besides the patriarchal diocese, there are five Archbishoprics, seven Bishoprics, and Vicariates in various countries. The Melkite Catholics number about 229,000 in all.

STRUCTURE OF THE MASS

At the beginning of the Mass the priest, after the preparation of the elements, makes a large sign of the cross over the altar with the book of the Gospels. He next chants the litanies and makes the Lesser Entrance with the Gospel book. After the Trisagion, the Epistle is chanted by the reader, and the priest chants the Gospel at the Royal Doors. Two litanies follow, while the priest, making once more the sign of the cross over the altar with the Gospel book, raises and kisses it, leans it against the tabernacle, and unfolds the antimension.

After the dismissal of the catechumens follow the litanies of the Mass of the Faithful, the Hymn of the Cherubim with its prayer and incensing, and the Greater Entrance with chalice and paten, which have until this time been on the preparation table. They are then incensed. A petition litany and the Credo close the part of the Mass preceding the anaphora.

The latter is introduced by the Pauline formula of blessing, the *Sursum Corda, Gratias Agamus,* Preface, and *Sanctus.* The climax of the liturgy is the Consecration, with anamnesis and invocation of the Holy Ghost (epiclesis). Then come the hymn to our Lady, commemoration of the saints and the dead, and the petitions of the diptycha.

The Communion is preceded by a petition litany, followed by the Our Father. After the little elevation, the Host is divided into four parts. The upper part, on which the Name of Jesus is stamped, is put into the chalice. A little hot water is added ("Fervor of Faith").

Then follow the Communion of the priest and of the faithful, the transfer of the chalice to the preparation table, the litany of thanksgiving, final prayer, and dismissal blessing. The priest consumes what remains of the Sacred Species at the preparation table and makes his thanksgiving.

PARTICULAR POINTS

1. The liturgical language is Arabic; only a few Greek words have been retained from antiquity.

   Note: Catholics of the Byzantine rite normally celebrate Mass in five principal languages: Greek, Old Slavonic, Arabic, Georgian, and Rumanian. To these must be added also Hungarian and, more rarely, other languages, including English.

2. Like the old Byzantine form of liturgy, the Melkite Mass has the same character as the Old Slavonic one; it differs, however, from the Old Slavonic in various details of the ceremony, in which Syrian influence is probably present.

   a. At the close of the Preface ("Cherubim and Seraphim") and of the epiclesis, the priest takes the folded small veil of the chalice and waves it several times in a circle over the Holy Gifts.

   b. During the Creed the priest holds the large veil by one end so that it hangs vertically, while he waves it back and forth over the Holy Gifts.

   c. As a sign that the Holy Gifts are the source of blessing, the priest makes the sign of the cross between chalice and paten. On another occasion, he touches the paten on which the already consecrated Host lies, before giving the blessing.

   d. During the Preface and the two petition litanies the priest extends his arms in a gesture of prayer.

   e. The paten used for the Mass is flat (but with a rim)—a discos without the foot.

   f. The leavened altar bread is in the form of a flat square, so molded as to facilitate its being broken into thin oblong particles.

   g. In distributing Communion, the priest takes one of these particles by one end, and dips the other end into the precious Blood, and so gives Communion.

   h. On weekdays (other than feasts) the Lesser and Greater Entrances are made in a simplified manner; the incensation also is somewhat different.

THE BLESSING OF THE ALTAR WITH THE GOSPEL BOOK

After the Holy Gifts have been readied on the altar of preparation (Proskomidi), and when the incensing has been performed and the intial solemn prayer, "Heavenly King . . ." recited, the priest makes the sign of the cross on the altar with the Gospel Book, saying: "Blessed be the Kingdom of the Father and of the Son and of the Holy Ghost, now and ever and unto ages of ages."

THE UNFOLDING OF THE ANTIMENSION

During the Litany of the Catechumens the priest prays: "O ye faithful, let us pray for the catechumens . . . that with us they may glorify Thy most honorable and august Name [unfolding the antimins], O Lord our God . . . look upon Thy servants, the catechumens . . . grant them forgiveness of their sins . . . unite them to the Holy Church. . . ."

PRAYER AFTER THE LITANY OF THE FAITHFUL

"We thank Thee, O Lord God of the Heavenly Hosts, that Thou hast vouchsafed us to stand, at this time, before Thy holy altar. We thank Thee that, from the exceeding greatness of Thy mercy, we may fall down before Thee to atone for our sins, and for as much as the people have through negligence offended.

"Graciously accept our petition and make us worthy to offer unto Thee prayers and supplications and this Unbloody Sacrifice."

INCENSING OF THE OFFERINGS

In solemn entrance, the priest has brought the Holy Gifts to the altar. Now he incenses them and prays: "Deal favorably, according to Thy good pleasure, O Lord, with Zion; build Thou the walls of Jerusalem. Then shalt Thou be pleased with the sacrifices of righteousness, with burnt offerings and holocausts."

END OF THE PREFACE—
THE STRIKING OF THE DISCOS WITH THE ASTERISK

"We thank Thee also for this ministry which Thou dost deign to accept from our hands, albeit there stand before Thee thousands of archangels and myriads of angels . . . who sing, cry out, and proclaim. . . ." [At these words the priest strikes the edge of the discos with the asterisk in four places.]

Thereafter follows the Sanctus, and immediately the Consecration.

CONSECRATION OF THE BREAD

The priest takes the bread, blesses it, and puts it down again. Then he holds his hands outstretched in blessing over the discos and pronounces the words of consecration: "Take and eat, this is My Body, which is broken for you for the forgiveness of sins."

Then the priest crosses himself and, with a deep bow, blesses the chalice forthwith; and holding his hand outstretched in blessing over it, says: "Drink ye all of it. . . ."

FRACTION OF THE SACRED HOST

Before Holy Communion, the priest breaks the Sacred Host into four pieces, which he replaces on the discos in the form of a cross, saying: "Broken and divided is the Lamb of God; broken yet undivided, eaten and not consumed, but sanctifying as many as partake thereof."

The priest drops the upper piece, signed with the name of Jesus, into the chalice. After Communion follows the Litany of Thanksgiving, the final blessing, and the Postcommunion of the priest.

SOLEMN MELKITE MASS IN ST. PETER'S

Concelebration—during the reading of the Epistle.

VIII. THE RUSSIAN LITURGY

HISTORY

The apostles of the Slavs, St. Cyril (d. 869) and St. Methodius (d. 885), were two brothers, of Greek origin, born in what is now Saloniki in Macedonia. While still layfolk, they received a philosophical and theological education; and Methodius, especially, took an active part in the administration of the Slavic regions of Macedonia. They thus learned the Slavic language in its Bulgarian dialect, even provided it with an alphabet of its own and translated into Bulgarian parts of the Bible and some of the liturgical books of the Greek (Byzantine) rite.

They felt themselves called to missionary activity among the Slavs, and went, presumably with a Greek embassy, into Southern Russia, where they were able to work for a while among the heathen Chazars.

At the request of Prince Rostislav of Moravia, who was eager to free his country from dependence upon the Frankish Empire, and to have Byzantine missionaries for his Slavic people, the Greek Emperor sent him the two brothers, Cyril (who was at that time still a layman, with the name Constantine) and Methodius, already a monk; and they converted the Moravians to Christianity and worked among them with great success. Since, with authorization from Rome, they celebrated the Latin Mass in the Slavic language, not only the Empire, but also the German bishops were discontented, and put the greatest obstacles in the way of their missionary labors. Methodius was consecrated bishop in Rome, and appointed Archbishop of Moravia. After a further sixteen years of labor and hardship, Methodius died in Velehrad in the year 885; Cyril had died in 869 on the occasion of the visit to Rome, having shortly before his death become a monk.

After Methodius' death, the Slavic Mass was suppressed in Moravia; and therefore the saintly Archbishop's disciples immigrated to Southern Slavic lands, where Old Slavonic had become the ecclesiastical language of the Byzantine liturgy. Russia also received the liturgy in this tongue, and in the Cyrillic alphabet. The two saints are justly venerated as the first apostles of the Slavs.

The Russian people embraced Christianity under the leadership of their Prince, St. Vladimir of Kiev, a grandson of the Princess, St. Olga. The leading members of the Varangian ruling class and many of the common folk were baptized, along with their prince, on the bank of the Dnieper. With the growth of the Russian Empire, Christianity also spread gradually to all the Slavic tribes. Russia had received Christianity, bishops, and the Byzantine liturgy from Constantinople, the ancient Byzantium, and was for that reason subject to the Patriarch of Constantinople. With mainly Greek archbishops and bishops as her leaders, Russia became more and more hostile toward Rome and the Catholic West; and after the Greek

Church had broken completely with Rome after 1054, Russia too was later drawn into this momentous schism.

The repeated attempts of the Popes to secure a reunion (especially at the Councils of Lyons, 1274, and Ferrara-Florence, 1439, with the mission of the Russian Catholic Metropolitan Isidore of Kiev) all came to nothing. When the Turks took Constantinople in 1583, the Russian Church declared itself autocephalous, that is, independent of the Patriarch of Constantinople, and self-governing. In the year 1589 the Metropolitan of Moscow was given the title of Patriarch, but in the eighteenth century Peter the Great abolished the Patriarchate.

There were in Russia previous to the Bolshevik revolution Russian Catholic communities of the Old Slavonic rite in the principal cities. These have perished. There were also some Russian thinkers during the last century who became acquainted with the Catholic Church abroad and became Catholics, for example, the celebrated philosopher Soloviev. Only a few of the Russians who left the country after the late war and the preceding one have gone over to Catholicism. Several Catholic spiritual centers have been founded, and in Rome the Russian College works at the formation of Catholic priests for future missionary work in Russia. Along with priests of all the Eastern rites, they receive a scientific foundation in the neighboring Oriental Institute.

STRUCTURE OF THE MASS

The priest on entering the church says certain prayers before the iconostasis, bows to the ground in reverence before the altar, and goes to the sacristy where he vests. During the preparation of the elements (Proskomidia) he cuts the altar bread. Leaving the preparation table, he incenses the altar and the icons of the sanctuary, the iconostasis, the church, and the people.

The Mass is preceded by a solemn introductory prayer, during which the priest raises his arms in prayer and bows low three times, making the sign of the cross. Then follow the introductory sign of the cross with the book of the Gospels, a Greater Litany and two Lesser Litanies, and the Lesser Entrance with the Gospel book.

After the Epistle, chanted by the reader, and the Gospel, sung by the priest, the Royal Doors are shut; after a series of litanies they are again opened for the Greater Entrance with chalice and paten, with which the priest blesses the people; then the Royal Doors are again closed. The Preface and *Sanctus* follow the Creed.

Next comes the Consecration with the anamnesis, an elevation of the Sacred Species and the invocation of the Holy Ghost (epiclesis), then the solemn commemoration of our Lady and the saints and the petitions (diptychs) for Pope and bishop.

With a litany of petition and the Our Father the Eucharistic Banquet begins:

a prayer with bowed head and another prayer, a little elevation of the Host, the fraction and the placing of a particle in the chalice, the infusion into the chalice of hot water, and the priest's Communion. The consecrated Host, the *Agnus Dei,* is divided into particles which are placed in the chalice, leaving on the paten the remaining particles.

After the Communion of the faithful, the remaining (unconsecrated) particles are put in the chalice, which is then taken to the preparation table. Then follow a litany of thanksgiving, a prayer read before the Royal Doors, and the last blessing. The priest consumes what remains of the Sacred Species at the preparation table and makes his thanksgiving.

PARTICULAR POINTS

1. The Proskomidia (preparation of the elements and first Offertory) takes place before the Mass begins. Generally five altar breads are used (sometimes only three). On them is stamped: I(esou)S NIKA; i.e., "Jesus Christ conquers." From one the stamped square is cut out to be consecrated, the *Agnus Dei.* From the others are cut particles to commemorate our Lady, the saints, the living and the dead. For this the priest uses a small lance. On the paten, to keep the veil from contact with the bread, is placed the asterisk, so called from the small star of Bethlehem which hangs from it. A spoon is used for giving Communion.

2. The Royal Doors (sometimes low and reticulated, allowing the altar to be seen through them) remain closed during the Mass, except for three occasions on which they are opened: (a) for the Lesser Entrance and the Trisagion, Epistle, incensation, and Gospel; (b) for the third incensation and the Greater Entrance with chalice and paten; (c) from the Communion of the faithful to the end.

3. The curtain of the Royal Doors is drawn open after the Proskomidia for the first incensation, and is drawn to again (an ancient usage in all the Eastern liturgies): (a) during the litany of petition after the Greater Entrance, and during the Kiss of Peace which follows when more than one priest celebrate together; (b) during the little elevation ("*Sancta Sanctis*"), the fraction and the placing of the particle in the chalice, the infusion of hot water ("Warmth of the Holy Ghost"), the priest's Communion, and the preparation of the particles for distribution.

4. The priest's attitude of prayer is an erect stance, with arms generally hanging naturally beneath the vestment. For certain prayers he raises his arms. The sign of the cross accompanied by a bow (poklon) is made on many occasions. There are no genuflections; only at the Our Father, on weekdays, does the priest pray kneeling.

5. At the Credo the priest holds the veil horizontal on both arms and moves it up and down over chalice and paten until the words ". . . and in the Holy Ghost."
6. At the final words of the Preface the priest makes the sign of the cross over the paten with the asterisk, folds the latter, signs himself with it, kisses it, and lays it aside.
7. There are ten litanies: the initial greater litany and two lesser ones, the "insistent" litany after the Gospel, the litany for the catechumens, and two short litanies for the faithful, the Anaphora litany after the Greater Entrance, the Communion litany before the Our Father, and the thanksgiving litany after the Communion. Where there is a deacon, it is he who sings the litanies.
8. In addition to the Liturgy of St. John Chrysostom, as above described, the Slavic rite has also the Liturgy of St. Basil and that of the Presanctified.

HUMILITY BEFORE GOD

First the priest says his preparatory prayers and makes reverence to the holy pictures on the iconostasis. Then, on entering the sanctuary, overcome by the holiness of the ever-present God, he falls upon his face in holy fear.

PREPARATION (PROSKOMIDIA)

From a small loaf of leavened bread, the priest, at the altar of preparation, cuts out a particle which symbolizes the Lamb of God, and smaller particles, in memory of those who stood on Golgatha at the foot of the cross, and of all those who now take their place beneath the cross in the Unbloody Sacrifice of the Holy Mass.

He prays: "In memory of our Lord, God and Saviour, Jesus Christ . . . He was led as a lamb to the slaughter . . . one of the soldiers pierced His side. . . ."

He lays a particle to the right of the *Agnus Dei* particle, saying: "In honor of our Most Blessed Sovereign, Mother of God and ever-virgin Mary. Accept, O Lord, by her intercession, this offering upon Thine altar beyond the sky. At Thy right hand stands the Queen, in a vesture of gold, gleaming in glory."

INCENSING OF ICONS

"We bow down before Thy Holy Icon, O Most Merciful One; and we implore forgiveness of our sins, O Christ Our God. For Thou didst deign, of Thy Providence, to go up unto the cross, in the flesh, that Thou mightest redeem them that Thou hadst created, from the bondage of the enemy; wherefore we do cry out in thanksgiving to Thee: Thou hast filled creation with gladness when Thou camest to save the world.

"We offer unto Thee this incense, O Christ, Our God. May it ascend as a pleasing ghostly savor even unto Thine altar in heaven, and do Thou send down to us from thence the grace of Thy Holy Spirit."

Before the beginning of the Liturgy proper, before the Gospel, and before the beginning of the sacrificial portion of the Mass, the priest incenses sanctuary, icons, and people, to prepare them worthily for the coming of God in word and sacrament.

SOLEMN ENTRY WITH THE GOSPEL

"Grant, O Lord, that this, our going in, may be accompanied by Thy Holy Angels; and that they may succor and support us in this service and with us praise Thy exceeding mercy; for to Thee belongeth all glory and honor and worship. . . ."

In solemn procession, the priest carries the Gospel Book, the symbol of the Word of God, through the Royal Doors to the altar.

OPENING OF THE ROYAL DOORS BEFORE SOLEMN ENTRY
WITH THE OFFERINGS

"We who do here the cherubim
Mystically represent and sing
To the life-giving Trinity
Praise in the great thrice holy hymn,
All of the cares that earth betide—
All of them let us now lay aside."

"Drink ye all of this; this is my Blood of the New Testament, which is shed for you and for many for the remission of sins."

By these words the priest, acting for the High Priest Eternal, achieves the miracle of transubstantiation.

Thereafter the priest says: "Mindful, therefore, of this salutary precept and of all that for our sakes did come to pass: the cross, the third day resurrection, the ascent into heaven, the sitting at the right hand of the Father, the second and glorious coming. . . ."

The priest now elevates both Sacred Species, makes with them the sign of the cross over the altar, and continues: "Thine Own, from what is already Thine, do we offer unto Thee for all manner of men and for all their necessities."

OUR FATHER

"For Thine is the Kingdom and the Power and the Glory, Father, Son, and Holy Ghost, now and ever and unto ages of ages."

The priest kneels on ferial days when pronouncing this greatest of prayers. On Sundays and feast days, however, he stands. Standing is, for the Byzantine, the attitude of supreme reverence. Kneeling partakes, rather, of the spirit of penance.

113

THE ADMIXTURE OF HOT WATER

"The fervor of faith, full of the Holy Ghost." The priest pours a few drops of hot water, which he has blessed, into the chalice, to signify the union, in faith, of our humanity with Christ.

SOLEMN FINAL BLESSING (ONE PRIEST)

"Christ, who didst rise from the dead, our True God, by the prayers of His Most Pure Mother, of the Holy and Blessed Apostles . . . and all the Saints, have mercy upon us and save us, for He is gracious and the Lover of mankind." With these words, the priest gives the blessing with the cross, after which, in commemoration of the early Christian agape, blessed bread (antidoron) is distributed to the faithful.

SOLEMN FINAL BLESSING

Three concelebrating priests are shown (of whom the first—holding the cross—is a "protoiereus"), the deacon (beside the first celebrant), and three acolytes.

IX. THE RUTHENIAN LITURGY

HISTORY

In the Western Ukraine, several Ruthenian (Ukrainian) dioceses were united with Rome by the Union of Brest in 1596, under the aegis of the Polish occupation; and several other dioceses joined them in 1700. The partition of Poland restored a great part of the Western Ukraine to Russian rule. The Russian sovereigns, especially Catherine II and Nicolas I, entirely abolished the Catholic hierarchy and forced the faithful in cruel fashion into Orthodoxy. In the districts allotted to Austria, the Catholic Ukrainians were able to maintain their faith undisturbed.

After the Russian edict of toleration of 1905, many Ukrainians (about 500,-000) returned to the Catholic Church. The Ukrainian Catholic Church was able to reorganize under the wise leadership of its great Metropolitan, Andrew Szeptyckyj, of Lvov, especially after the greater part of its territory had been partitioned between Czechoslovakia and Poland after the first World War. This Church had, on the eve of the second World War, five Bishoprics, an Apostolic Administratorship, and an Apostolic Visitor for Volhynia. The ecclesiastical province was governed by ten bishops and an Administrator Apostolic. Their auxiliaries in the care of souls numbered about 3,000 secular and over 600 regular clergy, with over 1,100 nuns. The Ukrainian Catholics then numbered about 4,300,000.

The outcome of the second World War delivered this most numerous Catholic community of the Eastern rite into terrible tribulation. Only a month after the end of the war (May 11, 1945) the entire Ukrainian Catholic hierarchy was arrested, and the people were forced to fall away from Rome. Thirty per cent of the clergy went over to Orthodoxy under the pressure of persecution; some twenty per cent fled abroad.

The Ukrainian Catholic Church in exile has four dioceses in Canada, three dioceses in the U.S.A., one Exarch in Australia, one Exarch in England, one bishop in Brazil, and one Exarch in Germany, while the rest of Western Europe is administered by an Apostolic Visitor. Working under the leadership of the bishops are 754 secular and 277 regular priests and 682 nuns (as of 1955). The number of Ukrainian emigrants (almost all Catholic) is more than a million and a quarter, most of them living in Canada and the U.S.A.

STRUCTURE OF THE MASS

During the preparation of the elements the priest symbolizes the sacrificial death of Christ by piercing the host, held in his left hand, with the lance.

After the preparation he goes to the altar, makes the Byzantine sign of the cross with three fingers and a bow, and begins the introductory prayer: "Heavenly King."

During the Mass of the Catechumens and after the first litanies occur the Lesser Entrance with the Gospel-book, the Trisagion, and the Epistle and Gospel. At the end of the prayer for the catechumens the priest spreads on the altar a Roman corporal, while the Byzantine antimension lies underneath the altar cloths.

As at the beginning of the Mass and during the reading of the Epistle, the priest incenses the altar, the Holy Gifts, the sanctuary, the iconostasis, and the people, before the Greater Entry. He then recites the Hymn of the Cherubim, and at the Greater Entry holds up the chalice and paten before the people, but without blessing the people with them. The Creed closes the part of the Mass prior to the anaphora.

After the Preface comes the Consecration, with anamnesis, followed by an elevation of the Sacred Species, and epiclesis (invocation of the Holy Ghost). Then follow the commemorations of our Lady and of the saints, and the diptycha.

The Communion is introduced by the Lord's Prayer. Then follow the elevation of the Host with the words, *"Sancta Sanctis,"* the fraction, and the Communions of the priest and of the faithful. The transfer of what remains of the Sacred Species to the preparation table, the dismissal blessing, and the consumption of the Sacred Species conclude the Mass.

PARTICULAR POINTS

1. The daily Mass is for the most part merely spoken, and without incensation.
2. In most cases a Greek paten without a foot is used.
3. The leavened altar bread is in ready-made form as a host about 4 cm. square and 1 cm. thick, without any stamp. The particles for our Lady, the saints, the living and the dead, are likewise ready-cut.
4. Hence, at the preparation, the cutting out of the Host is performed only symbolically, by drawing the lance along the sides of the Host.
5. When preparing the host, the priest takes it in his left hand; he turns it with the lance and pierces it on one side of the upper surface.
6. All the particles on the paten are consecrated, are put into the chalice before the Communion, and are distributed.
7. The Byzantine antimension lies permanently under the two upper altar-cloths.
8. The Mass vestment is cut close to the shoulders, and is longer in front, but shorter at the back than the Russian.
9. It is not the custom to bow and sign oneself at individual petitions of the litanies, but all make the sign of the cross at the priest's "Peace be to all."
10. In prayer the hands are either stretched forth or joined at the breast.

11. There is no threefold raising of the hands in prayer before the epiclesis.
12. Hot water is not blessed and put in the chalice.
13. At the Greater Entry the priest pronounces only the close of the formula of commemoration toward the people, and gives no blessing.
14. During the Creed the priest holds the veil by one end and waves it hanging vertically before the chalice.
15. After distributing Communion, the priest puts the paten on the altar and blesses the people with the chalice.
16. The Royal Doors of the iconostasis remain open during the whole ceremony.

PIERCING WITH THE LANCE

"One of the soldiers pierced His side with a lance, and straightway there poured forth blood and water; he that saw it hath borne witness to it and his witness is true."

The priest then pours wine and water into the chalice and places to the left of the Host a particle in honor of our Lady, who stood beneath the cross; to the right of it he places particles in honor of the Heavenly Hosts and the saints, and below it particles for the living and the dead.   121

SIGN OF THE CROSS

"Heavenly King, Comforter and Spirit of Truth, come and abide in us and cleanse us from every stain; and save, Most Merciful, our souls."

Several times during the Holy Liturgy, the priest crosses himself in humble reverence before God and invokes the redeeming power of the cross of Christ.

ANTIMENSION

"O Lord our God, that dwellest on the highest heaven and lookest down upon the least of Thy creatures: to save mankind Thou hast sent Thine only begotten Son, God our Lord, Jesus Christ. Look down now with eyes of mercy upon Thy servants, the catechumens. Grant them in due season the laver of regeneration, forgiveness of sins, and the robe of incorruption. Join them to Thy Holy Catholic and Apostolic Church and number them among Thine elect, that they too, along with us, may join in the praises of Thine all-holy and majestic name, Father and Son and Holy Ghost, now and for ever, and for all eternity. Amen."

During the dismissal of the catechumens the priest spreads the Roman corporal. The Byzantine antimension (as in the illustration), containing relics of the saints, remains permanently underneath the altar cloth.

HYMN OF THE CHERUBIM

Before the Greater Entrance with chalice and paten, the priest says the prayer: "No one who is bound with the desires and pleasures of the flesh is worthy to approach or draw nigh to serve Thee, O King of Glory; for to serve Thee is a great and terrible thing even to the Heavenly Powers. . . ."

Before the incensation of the altar, the Holy Gifts, the sanctuary, the iconostasis, and the faithful, the priest says three times the Hymn of the Cherubim, each time raising his arms to heaven and then bowing with a sign of the cross.

GREATER ENTRY WITH THE OFFERINGS

"May the Lord God remember in his Kingdom, His Holiness the Universal Pastor . . . Pope and Bishop of Rome . . . our most reverend archbishop, priests, deacons, the clergy regular, and all Orthodox Christians." At these final words the priest turns toward the people, and thereupon carries the Holy Gifts (prepared for the accomplishment of the Sacrifice, but not yet consecrated) through the Royal Doors to the altar.

ELEVATION OF THE SACRED SPECIES

Immediately after the words of institution and the anamnesis, the priest elevates the Sacred Species in the sign of the cross and says: "Thine own of Thine own we offer unto Thee, on behalf of all and for all."

RUTHENIAN PONTIFICAL

The deacon kisses the cross before reading the Gospel. Deacon: "Bless, Sir, the herald of the holy Apostle and Evangelist. . . ." Bishop: "May God, by the prayers of the holy, glorious, and all-praiseworthy Apostle and Evangelist . . . give unto thee speech, as thou proclaimest good news with much strength, for the fulfillment of the Gospel of His beloved Son, Jesus Christ our Lord."

X. THE CHALDEAN LITURGY

HISTORY

The Chaldeans are the Oriental Christians of the East Syrian, i.e., the Chaldean rite. They are descended from the pre-Christian Chaldeans (Assyrian and other Babylonian tribes) who, in the course of time, intermingled with the original inhabitants of Kurdistan. They live, today, chiefly in Iraq and in the neighborhood of Mosul.

Christianity penetrated from Edessa in Syria, via Mesopotamia, to the Chaldeans and Assyrians, and beyond the Tigris, where there existed numerous, flourishing Jewish settlements which became the bearers of Christianity. According to ancient tradition, St. Thomas the Apostle worked among them as a missionary.

A constant stream of new missionaries and bishops (and Jewish refugees from Rome-besieged Palestine) kept flowing in from Edessa and organized the Chaldean Church, which spread southward among the Persians.

The perpetual wars of the Persians with the Romans rendered the ecclesiastical relations with the West Syrian bishops very difficult. The long and cruel persecution of the Christians by the Persian state, which wanted to help the old heathen religion of fire-worship to victory over newly arisen Christianity, made it imperative to avoid the slightest suspicion of liaison with the Syrian national enemy. Thus it came about that the Chaldeans dissolved their dependence (tenuous though it was) from the newly rising Patriarch of Antioch and, in 424, declared themselves independent in the ecclesiastical administration of the Chaldean Church of Persia.

Notwithstanding bloody persecutions, the Christian Church of Persia grew tremendously after religious freedom had been regained. Likewise under the Arabs, who conquered Persia in 642, the Chaldean Church carried its zealous missionary work to the farthest corners of Asia. She had won nearly fifty million adherents by the thirteenth century, who were scattered over 230 dioceses, extending to Mongolia, China, and South India.

In the fourteenth century, sudden ruin overwhelmed this flourishing Church, which had spread over the whole of Asia. The raging hordes of the Mongol, Tamerlane, passed over it, and only a pitiful remnant of the ancient Church remained. The Occidental portion of the Chaldean Christians grouped themselves round their Katholikos (Patriarch) in Northern Mesopotamia. Of the Oriental portion, only the Chaldean Malabarese in South India were left.

Unfortunately, the Chaldean (Persian) Church had no longer been Catholic after the end of the fifth century. For it had separated itself, even in dogma, at the Synod of Seleucia, in 486, from the Greek Church, and therewith from the Universal Church, and had become Nestorian, i.e., it taught two persons in Christ. In the thirteenth century, a number of Chaldean Patriarchs of Baghdad united themselves to the Catholic Church, thanks to the missionary work of the Dominicans. In 1445, a Chaldean archbishop in Cyprus became Catholic and brought all his faithful with him.

With the year 1551 began, for those Chaldeans reunited with Rome, the line of the Catholic Chaldean Patriarchs, who bear the title "Patriarch of Babylon." Under their second last Patriarch, Mar Emmanuel Thomas (d. 1947), a solid group of about 20,000 Nestorians came over to the Catholic Church.

In Khabur there is a new Catholic mission (Redemptionist) to the 12,000 abandoned Nestorians who are under the Chaldean Catholic Bishop Naamo in Beirut.

The Catholic Patriarch of the Chaldeans administers thirteen dioceses (mostly in Iraq) with 196,000 Catholics of the Chaldean rite. There are today 70,000 Nestorians.

During the bloody Turkish butcheries of 1914-18 many Catholic and Nestorian Chaldeans were annihilated.

STRUCTURE OF THE MASS

After a prayer at the foot of the altar, the priest prays antiphonally with the server the Thanksgiving (Lakhu Mara), offers bread and wine, and prays the Trisagion.

When the server has read the Epistle, the priest reads the Gospel. At the same spot, in the middle of the sanctuary, he says the prayer for the catechumens (Karozutha) and the Prayer of the Laying on of Hands.

After the dismissal of the catechumens the Mass of the Faithful begins, with the Washing of Hands and Second Offertory, which is also a memento of the Lord, His Blessed Mother, the saints, and the faithful departed. In the center of the sanctuary again, the Entry Prayer and Creed are said; then follows the Great Entry, a solemn progress to the altar, interrupted by three deep bows and concluding with a veneration of the altar (three genuflections, kissing the altar each time). The Kiss of Peace of the Canon is followed by the representation of the tomb, the Preface, *Sanctus,* Prayer of *Sanctus,* and consecration, with adoration after the Consecration. There is now no anamnesis, but there are intercessions (Diptycha) and invocation of the Holy Ghost (epiclesis).

The Eucharistic Banquet begins, for the Chaldeans, not with the Our Father, but with the first elevation of the Sacred Host, after the priest has given thanks for the accomplishment of the Sacrifice and has confessed, before God, his unworthiness to approach the Holy Banquet. After the fraction and the intinction follows the Great Elevation of the Sacred Host. Thereafter follow the Communion Prayer, the Our Father, the *Sancta Sanctis,* and the showing of the Sacred Species. After the Absolution and Communion come the thanksgiving and blessing.

PARTICULAR POINTS

1. The sanctuary is a chapel, enclosed by high walls, with a door. At all times other than those of the Holy Sacrifice, and for certain periods even of it, the curtain of this door is closed.
2. The First Offertory of bread and wine occurs after the Prayer of Thanksgiving (Lakhu Mara).
3. Low Mass is a silent Mass, without incensing.
4. In most cases, the sign of the cross, genuflections, form of the host, the priest's Communion, and the distribution of Communion to the faithful are of Latin provenience.
5. The host, however, is of leavened bread.
6. Initial words or phrases are often repeated two or three times, to express the insistence of the prayer.
7. The ever-recurring motif is praise of Christ, who is the resurrection of the body and the Saviour of souls.
8. More than thirty acts of trusting humility and contrition before the awe-inspiring Majesty of God are included in the Mass liturgy.
9. Notably frequent are the genuflections, particularly before the Consecration.
10. In the middle of the sanctuary occur: Karozutha, prayer for the elect, Prayer of the Laying on of Hands, Entry Prayer, and Creed. After this comes the Great Entry, with three bows to the altar.
11. The large sign of the cross, with blessing of the faithful, is repeated twice.
12. Symbolic of the tomb of the Lord is the folded chalice veil, which is wrapped round the sacred vessels, from the beginning of the Canon until after the elevation of the chalice.
13. The priest says twice only: "Peace be with you"; but the server says twelve times: "Peace be with us."
14. Quite unique is the position assumed by the priest on four occasions, before and after the consecration: praying, bowed deeply before the altar, his hands held out before him in an imploring gesture (e.g., Preface).
15. Also unique is the "showing," i.e., the reverent indication of the Sacred Species, coupled with a threefold *Agnus Dei, Qui tollis. . . .*
16. The spreading out and lowering of the Hands over the Sacred Gifts at the Invocation of the Holy Ghost (epiclesis) is unique.

17. The host remains on the paten at the consecration and is taken into the hand of the priest only at the elevation.
18. A solemn Our Father inaugurates and closes the Holy Mass. The Our Father of the Eucharistic Banquet occurs immediately before the Communion.
19. Places in church are allotted in a manner which goes back to the custom of the Jewish synagogue. The children's places are near the choir dais in front of the doors; behind them, in the middle portion of the church, are the men; and behind the men, and separated from them by a wooden lattice, are the women.
20. There is no anamnesis after the words of institution.
21. The Trisagion is pronounced by the server.

PRAYER TO THE THRICE HOLY (TRISAGION)

After the priest has for the first time offered the Gifts and given thanks to God, the servers pray the triple Kyrie: "Holy God, Holy Strong One, Holy Immortal One, have mercy upon us!"

Then the priest pronounces the Prayer of the Trisagion: "O Holy Glorious, Strong, Immortal God, who dwellest in the Holy Place, wherein Thy Will doth rest, we implore Thee: hear us, O Lord, have mercy upon us, as Thou art wont to do, O Lord of the World, Father, Son, and Holy Ghost."

Then the server kisses the priest's hand, receives his blessing, and advances to read the Epistle.

"O Christ, who art the glory and image of the Father, Thou hast appeared in the form of a man and hast lightened the darkness of our minds with the Light of Thy Gospel; we thank Thee, we worship Thee, we magnify Thee, forever, O Lord of the World. Make us wise, O Lord, with Thy Law; clarify our powers with Thy Wisdom; sanctify our souls with Thy Truth and make us docile to Thy Word and obedient to Thy commandments, forever and ever, O Lord of the World."

Thereafter the priest blesses the people with the Book and reads the Gospel.

PRAYER OF DISMISSAL OF CATECHUMENS (KAROZUTHA)

"O Lord, Mighty God, we pray Thee most heartily, fill us with Thy grace and pour forth Thy bounty. . . . May Thy compassion and the tender mercies of Thy Godhead grant unto Thy people pardon of guilt and to all the sheep of Thy flock that Thou hast chosen, forgiveness of sins, through Thy grace and compassion, O Lord of the World, Father, Son, and Holy Ghost, now and forever."

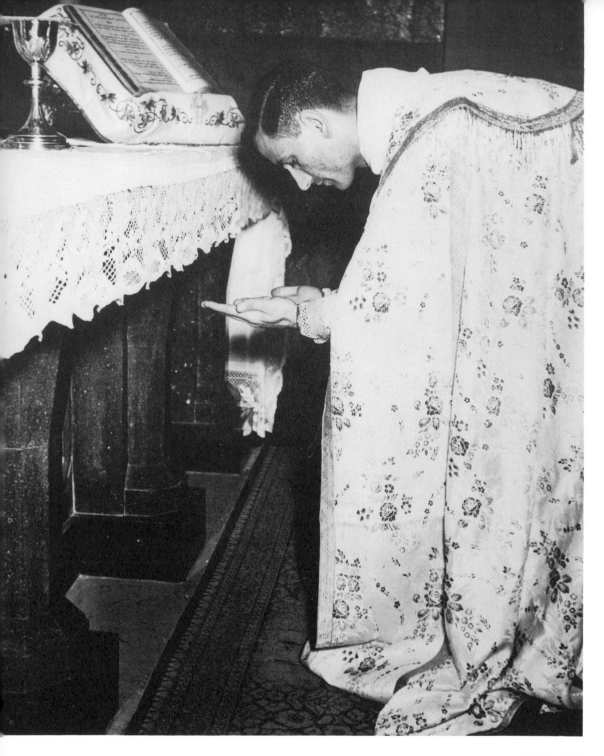

"It is meet and right that every mouth should praise, every heart give thanks, every creature worship and magnify the adorable and wonderful Name of the Glorious Trinity, who created us . . . sanctified . . . and redeemed us, Father, Son, and Holy Ghost. O Lord, legions of the blessed spirits do magnify Thy Name, together with the Cherubim and Seraphim, and do worship Thy Majesty."

The priest prays these introductory words of the Preface while bowed low before the altar. Then the Sanctus and Sanctus prayer are said in an erect position.

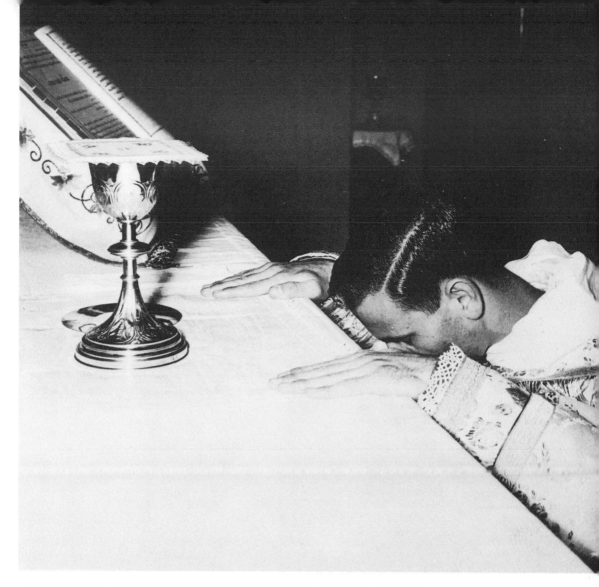

ADORATION AFTER THE CONSECRATION OF THE BREAD

"And as it was promised, we, Thy humble, weak, and miserable servants, are gathered together, for Thou hast granted us a great grace, inasmuch as Thou hast filled us men with Thy divine life and hast ministered to our weakness. Thou hast atoned for our fall and wakened us from the dead; our sins hast Thou forgiven and covered our guilt with a garment of righteousness; our conscience hast Thou enlightened and confounded our enemy, O Divine Lord. And so, in the exceeding great compassion of Thy grace, hast Thou favored our weakness with the victory."

INVOCATION OF THE HOLY GHOST (EPICLESIS)

The priest spreads out his hands, joins them above his head, and lowers them upon the Holy Gifts. He says aloud: "May Thy Holy Spirit descend!" and continues "O Lord, may Thy blessing descend upon this offering of Thy servants. Sanctify it, to the end that it may be for us unto pardon of our guilt, forgiveness of our sins, pledge of the resurrection of the dead, and new life in the Kingdom of Heaven. For all this great and wonderful dispensation of salvation we do thank Thee, and we praise Thee without ceasing, with unfeigned trust in Thee, in Thy Church, which hath been redeemed by the precious Blood of Thy Christ. To Thy Holy Name we offer honor and glory, praise and worship, now and for ever and ever."

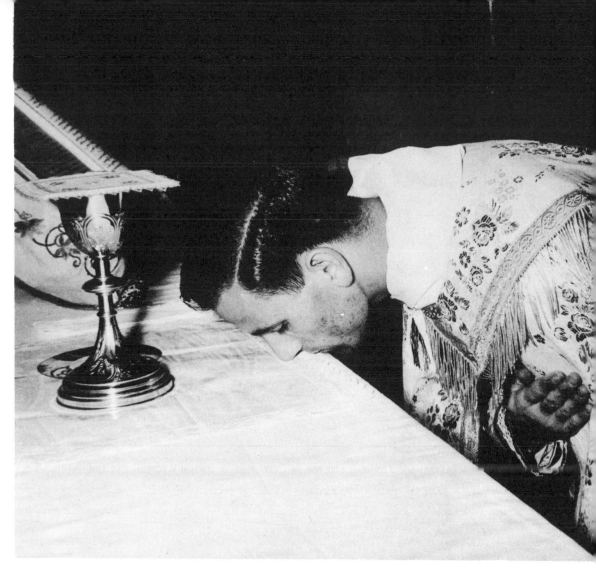

KISSING OF THE ALTAR

The priest concludes the sacrifice with a prayer for peace. Then he thanks God for the grace that he was granted to accomplish the sacrifice:

"I thank Thee, Father, Lord of heaven and earth, Son, and Holy Ghost, that Thou hast vouchsafed me, notwithstanding my sins and unworthiness, to offer up before Thee these dreadful, holy, lifegiving Divine Mysteries of the Body and Blood of Thy Christ and so to mediate unto Thy people and the sheep of Thy fold, pardon of their guilt, forgiveness of their sins, salvation of their souls, as well as atonement for the whole world, peace and quiet for all the churches.

"Bless us, O Lord; bless us, O Lord; bless us, O Lord! May Thy merciful loving kindness, O Lord and God, draw us near unto these lofty, holy, life giving, and Divine Mysteries, notwithstanding our unworthiness."

Server: "Yea, verily, notwithstanding our unworthiness!"

HOLY THINGS FOR THE HOLY

After the contrition and Communion prayers, the Our Father and the Invitation to the Sacrificial Banquet, the priest turns to the people, bows slightly, opens his hands in a gesture of invitation, and closes them with the words: "Holy Things for the Holy!"

PRESENTATION OF THE SACRED SPECIES AND AGNUS DEI

The priest shows the faithful the Sacred Host above the chalice. He retreats reverently, and strikes his breast, saying: "Lamb of God, Thou that takest away the sins of the world, grant us Thy pardon . . . O Son of God, Thou hast given us Thy Body and Thy Blood; vouchsafe unto us life in Thy Kingdom." Thereafter follow Communion, Thanksgiving, and Final Blessing.

141

OFFERING OF BREAD AND WINE

In the Mass of the Faithful, the announcement of the day's feast—the so-called "Onitha"—is sung twice, introducing the Offertory. Then the priest takes the chalice in his right hand and the paten in his left; crossing his arms and elevating his eyes to heaven, he raises the offerings and says, "O Lord, we glorify Thy glorious Trinity. . . . Christ has sacrificed himself for our salvation and has sent us to celebrate the memory of his death, burial, and resurrection. . . . May he accept graciously this sacrifice from our hands, for ever and ever, world without end."

XI. THE MALABARESE LITURGY

HISTORY

Tradition has it that St. Thomas brought the Christian message to India, along the Malabar coast (hence the name, "Thomas Christians"). Most probably, however, the Chaldean rite reached India via the Chaldean Christians who emigrated from Mesopotamia and Persia during the fourth and fifth centuries, at the time of the Persian persecution of the Christians.

When the Portuguese came to India about 1500, they found a body of Christians of the Chaldean rite, numbering over 100,000 souls. They were Indians whose ancestors, long in India, may have intermarried with the Chaldeans and with other immigrants of Arab origin. These Christians also had bishops, who were dependent on the Nestorian Patriarchs of Mesopotamia. Under pressure of the political situation, the Portuguese won them to the Catholic Church, but made the most unwise mistake of trying again and again, for 150 years, to Latinize them. Finally there developed a schism, in which almost all the Malabarese fell away from the Church. After ten years of unremitting effort, the Italian Carmelites succeeded in winning back over half of the Thomas Christians. The remaining portion united, in 1665, with the Syrian Jacobite Patriarchate of Antioch.

Since, in the course of time, a portion of the converted heathen Malabarese adopted the Latin rite, the Christians were split in three parts: Latin Catholics, Chaldean Catholics, and Syrian Jacobites. A group of 35,000 of these Jacobites came over in 1930 to the Catholic Church, under the leadership of their Archbishop Mar Ivanios of Trivandrum. These converts received the name "Malankars," to distinguish them from those Malabarese who still remained Jacobites. Their number has already grown to 108,000.

Since 1896, the Malabarese have had native bishops. Vocations among the Malabarese are so numerous that the Church can hope they will proselytize other Indian territories. The Chaldean Malabars have seven dioceses; the Latins also have seven. The youngest group—the Malankars—have two dioceses. Each group also has an archbishop. The present number of Chaldean Malabarese is 1,377,000.

These Thomas Christians are often called "Syro-Malabarese," although their rite is not Syrian, but a modified form of Chaldean, which since the Portuguese occupation of the Malabar Coast has been Latinized in many respects, principally in ceremonial details. A reform is to be undertaken.

STRUCTURE OF THE MASS

After a genuflection, the priest places the chalice on the altar, readies the Missal, and begins Holy Mass with the Prayer at the foot of the Altar; thereafter, he prays the Thanksgiving. Then follow a prayer, the Trisagion in the middle of the altar, the Epistle on the Epistle side, and the Gospel on the Gospel side. Then comes the Creed, the priest making three inclinations to the altar and kneeling once. Now the sacred vessels, veil, and pall are incensed. Wine and water are poured in, and a Litany is prayed.

After the Prayer of the Laying on of Hands, the Blessing and the Dismissal, the Mass of the Catechumens is over and the Mass of the Faithful begins. A symbolic translation of the Holy Gifts is accomplished, with the showing of the paten with the bread to the faithful. Thereafter the Offertory takes place, with first Mementos of our Lord, His Most Blessed Mother, the Angels, the saints, and the faithful departed. Then follow the Offertory Prayer and the veneration of the altar, now kissed fourteen times.

The Sacrifice begins with the Anaphora (Canon) and the Kiss of Peace, the priest making the Great Sign of the Cross over himself and the people. After the uncovering of the Holy Gifts and the symbolic representation of the tomb of our Lord, there follow Preface, *Sanctus,* long Intercessions (Diptycha), a second Memento of the Lord, Memento of His Most Blessed Mother, and invocation of the Holy Ghost.

With the Prayer of Penance and the incensing of the priest, the servers, the people, and the Holy Gifts, everything is prepared for the most solemn moment, the Consecration, which the priest now accomplishes.

After genuflection and elevation of the separate Holy Gifts follow immediately the breaking of Bread and the signing of one half of the Host by the other half, which has been dipped into the precious Blood. The tomb is now removed, since the union of the Species signifies the resurrection, and the priest makes the sign of our salvation upon his forehead. A Little Elevation of both Sacred Species follows.

The priest, with the Host in his left hand, says the *"Domine, non sum dignus"* and receives Holy Communion. After the Sacred Banquet of the Faithful comes the Thanksgiving and the Final Blessing.

PARTICULAR POINTS

1. Latin genuflections and Mass vestments are used.
2. There is no preparation of the Holy Gifts after the Prayers at the Foot of Altar, as in the Chaldean rite. (Herein the Malabarese are closer than the Chaldeans to the original rite.)

3. The Trisagion is prayed by the priest; in the Chaldean rite, it is said by the server.
4. The Latin position is observed during prayers; there is no "Prayer of Trisagion," as there is in the Chaldean rite.
5. Epistle and Gospel are according to the Latin fashion; in the Chaldean rite, the server reads the Epistle, and the priest, the Gospel.
6. The Creed is anticipated; in the Chaldean rite, it follows the Offertory in the Mass of the Faithful. Likewise anticipated is the Great Entry, accomplished during the Creed; in the Chaldean rite, it comes after the Creed and has a special prayer.
7. The Intercessions (Diptychs), anamnesis, epiclesis, and the Kiss of Peace are all anticipated; in the Chaldean rite they come only after the Consecration.
8. The Great Elevation of the Sacred Species, of the Host and Chalice, is anticipated to the point after each Consecration, corresponding to the Latin usage, with genuflection each time. In the Chaldean rite it comes only at the beginning of the Eucharistic Banquet.
9. Thanksgiving for the Sacrifice, combined with the Pauline Blessing, is a final prayer of the Sacrifice itself, but occurs only after the Signing of the Holy Host with the precious Blood.
10. The threefold *Agnus Dei* and the subjoined little elevation are in imitation of the Latin rite; in the Chaldean, instead, occur Karozutha, the general Prayer of Contrition, and the great Communion Prayer of the priest.
11. The *Sancta Sanctis* is even simpler than in the Chaldean rite.
12. There is the threefold *Domine non sum dignus* after the Latin fashion; in the Chaldean rite, on the other hand, an Ostension (showing of the Holy Gifts) with a threefold *Agnus Dei* takes place.
13. The forms of the Communion of the priest, and of the distribution of Communion to the faithful are Latin. This is also true of the Chaldean rite.
14. In all else the Malabarese liturgy is an adapted Chaldean rite, with Karozutha, Prayer of the Laying on of Hands, Dismissal of Catechumens, Offertory, mementos, and veneration of altar.
15. Especially peculiar to the Malabarese rite are the incensing of all the sacred instruments at the preparation for the Sacrifice (after the Creed), and the incensing of the priest, the servers, the people, and the Holy Gifts shortly before the Consecration.
16. For the restoration of the Malabarese liturgy, the following alterations are suggested: Oriental Mass vestments; Epistle, Gospel, and Inclination Prayers according to the Chaldean rite; Creed after Offering; Consecration before anamnesis and epiclesis; Inclinations instead of genuflections; partial use of the vernacular.

PRAYER AT THE FOOT OF THE ALTAR

"In the name of the Father . . . Holy, Holy, Holy is the Lord God of Hosts. Heaven and earth are full of His Glory, full of the presence of His Triune Consubstantiality, full of the radiance of His glorious beauty. Praise be to Thee, O Lord!"

THANKSGIVING AFTER THE PRAYER
AT THE FOOT OF THE ALTAR

"We praise Thee, Lord, for Thine unutterable succour and grace. We desire to magnify Thee without ceasing in Thy glorious Church, which is full of Thy favor and blessing, for Thou art the Lord and Creator of all things, Father, Son, and Holy Ghost, from eternity even unto eternity."

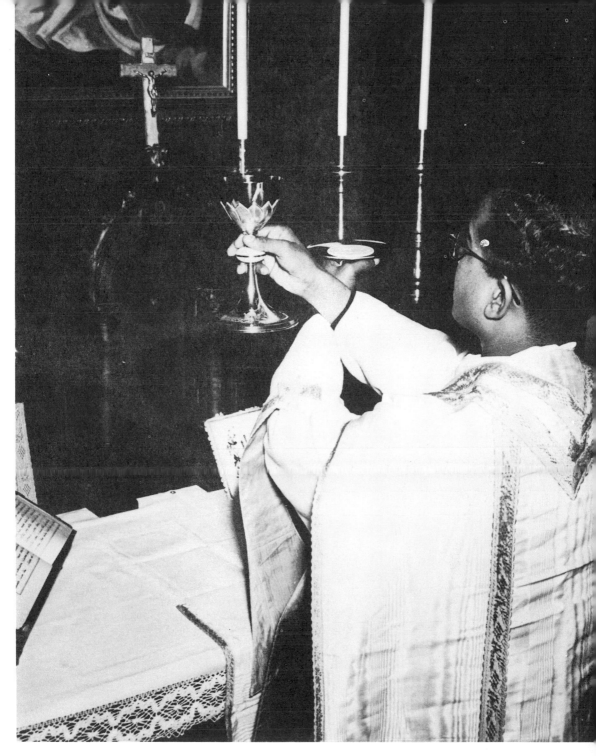

OFFERTORY

"Unto Thy glorious Trinity do we offer up honor forever. May the same Christ who was offered up for our salvation, and did command us to celebrate the remembrance of it, His passion, death, burial, and resurrection, accept this offering from our hands, through His eternal grace and goodness. Amen."

THE GREAT BLESSING AT THE BEGINNING OF THE CANON

"We are full of sin and frailty, but through the exceeding greatness of Thy mercy, Thou dost make us worthy to be servants of the Holy Mysteries of the Body and Blood of Christ. We implore Thine aid unto our strengthening, to the end that we may dispense in perfect love and true faith the Gifts that Thou hast entrusted unto us. To Thee be honor, glory, praise, and worship, forever and ever."

INVOCATION OF THE HOLY GHOST (EPICLESIS)

"May Thy Holy Spirit, O Lord, descend and rest upon this offering of Thy servants. May He bless it and sanctify it, to the end that it may be for us unto pardon of guilt and remission of our sins, a steadfast hope of the resurrection of the dead, unto a new life in the heavenly kingdom, with all those that rejoice in beholding Thy countenance."

CONSECRATION OF THE BREAD

In preparation for the consecration, the priest prays: "O Christ, who art the peace of the saints and the steadfast hope of sinners, confirm the whole world in peace and quietness, especially Thy Holy Catholic Church; protect us from war, and give peace in our time."

Then he pronounces the words of consecration and prays at the elevation of the Sacred Host: "Behold the living and life-giving Bread, that cometh down from heaven and giveth life to the whole world. As many as shall eat of it, shall not die; as many as partake of it, shall be saved and sanctified and shall have life eternal."

THE SIGN OF THE CROSS ON THE FOREHEAD
AFTER THE BREAKING OF BREAD

"Accomplished and united are the Divine Mysteries, in the Name of the Most Holy Trinity, unto the forgiveness of sins, the sure and certain hope of the resurrection of the dead and of new life in the kingdom of heaven."

MALABARESE PONTIFICAL
SHOWING OF HOST WITH OFFERTORY PRAYER

"With desire have I waited for the Lord"—said twice.

"With fear and trembling let us all offer unto Him as victim upon the holy altar, the Body of Christ and His precious Blood. Let us cry unto Him with the angels: 'Holy, holy, holy art Thou, Lord and God.' "

154

XII. THE ARMENIAN LITURGY

HISTORY

The Armenians are an Indo-European people, dwelling in the mountainous part of Asia Minor between the Taurus and Caucasus Mountains. Christianity penetrated into Armenia as early as the first century. At the end of the third century King Tiridates III was converted to Christianity by the bishop St. Gregory "the Illuminator" ("Enlightener"), and Christianity became the religion of the State.

Owing to the disturbed conditions caused by war, the Armenian bishops were not represented at the Council of Chalcedon (451), in which Monophysitism, that is, the false teaching that Christ's human nature was wholly absorbed by His divine nature, was condemned.

The inaccurate version which they received of the conciliar decisions led the Armenian bishops to reject the Council of Chalcedon, which they accused of

Nestorianism, that is, of teaching that there were two persons in Christ. The concepts of "nature" and "person," and their expression, were not at that time unambiguously clear, and frequently led to misunderstandings.

Thanks also to the national hostility to the Greeks, Monophysitism gradually penetrated into Armenia from Mesopotamia, and gained the upper hand. It so came about that in the sixth and seventh centuries the Armenian Church became more and more separated from the Catholic, and was henceforth accounted Monophysite.

At the time of the Crusades the Armenians, who had migrated westward and founded an Armenian kingdom in Cilicia, became Catholic; but after the Turkish invasion they fell back once more in 1375 into Monophysitism.

In the fourteenth century the Dominicans had founded Armenian Brotherhoods to work for reunion, but without attaining any lasting result until the seventeenth century, when numerous Armenians became Catholic. In 1701 the Armenian Catholic monk Mechitar founded an Armenian Order of the Benedictine type, which survives to our own day in Venice and Vienna (about fifty monks in each monastery, the "Mechitarists").

The Catholic Patriarchate of Cilicia began in 1740; the Patriarchs reside at Beirut, Lebanon.

In modern times (1915-1918) the Turks carried out in Asia Minor a cruel persecution of Christians, directed especially against the Armenians, many of whom perished, while many fled into exile. The majority of the Armenian Catholics now live in Syria and in the United States. Of the non-Catholic ("Gregorian") Armenians about a third live in Soviet Armenia, and the rest are scattered in Persia, Iraq, Syria, Lebanon, Egypt, and elsewhere; they are distributed among four Patriarchates.

There are 100,000 Catholic and 2,500,000 Gregorian Armenians, all, save for minor differences, with the same rite.

The series of photographs, taken in the Armenian church at Rome, represents the simple everyday liturgy of the Catholic Armenians.

STRUCTURE OF THE MASS

After the prayers at the foot of the altar steps, the priest goes up to the altar, and immediately makes the first Offertory, elevating chalice and paten, which he then covers and blesses.

Then follow the Introit of the day, "Peace be to all," and four prayers said in the center of the altar with outstretched arms, and the Trisagion. The priest then reads the Epistle—after the Latin manner—from the Missal, but the Gospel from the Gospel book, at the Gospel side of the altar, facing the people, first blessing the people with the words "Peace be to all." At the words of the Creed "and became flesh" he genuflects.

The Mass of the Faithful begins with the second Offertory and goes on until the Kiss of Peace.

In the anaphora, the Preface and the great Sanctus Prayer are followed at once by the consecration, with anamnesis, gesture of humility and thanksgiving, and epiclesis (invocation of the Holy Ghost). Then follow the lengthy commemorations of Pope and Bishop, living and dead, the poor, the sick, the imprisoned, together with those of our Lady and the saints.

The Communion is preceded by the Our Father, after which follow the Prayer of the Laying on of Hands, that is, of special blessing, the elevation of the sacred Host and of the chalice, along with a blessing, imparted with the chalice, with the Host held over the chalice; this serves at the same time as the invitation to the Communion.

After preparatory prayers, priest and faithful communicate; the Mass closes with a Last Gospel and a prayer with the last blessing.

PARTICULAR POINTS

1. The Armenians' oldest liturgy was the Syrian one of Caesarea in Cappadocia. After the development in the fifth century of Armenian literature, the Scriptures and the liturgical books were translated into Armenian. The liturgy was at the same time brought into closer agreement with the Byzantine liturgies of St. John Chrysostom and St. Basil. The Armenian liturgy as such was formed in the sixth and seventh centuries, in the golden age of national literature, by the addition of original hymns, prayers, and customs, which made of it a distinct rite. Nevertheless, even today many prayers of the Armenian liturgy are evidently literal translations from the Byzantine liturgy.
2. There is only the one redaction of the liturgy, and the one anaphora form, all the year round. There is a completely silent ("Low") Mass, and a very solemn form of High Mass, with as many as six deacons, and with a fuller form of the same redaction of the liturgy.
3. At High Mass even simple priests wear, at the beginning and end of the ceremony, a crown shaped mitre.
4. During the prayers at the foot of the altar, the priest, after the server's *Confiteor,* turns toward the people to give the absolution.
5. The structure of the Mass after the Gospel is peculiar to this rite: there are the Creed with an exorcism of heretics, a prayer for the gifts of the Holy

157

Ghost, anamnesis, and prayer for peace as parts of the Mass of the Catechumens, while that of the Faithful is made up principally of Offertory prayers and the second Offertory.

6. There are two Offertory elevations: one at the beginning of the Mass, and the second, with a longer Offertory prayer, before the Canon.

7. On both occasions the priest elevates the chalice with the paten, upon which lies the Host; this is to be found only in the Armenian rite.

8. The hosts are unleavened and like Roman ones; distribution of Communion also is on the Latin model, but with different prayer formulas.

9. The Preface has the common Eastern structure: after the Pauline formula of blessing, the *Sursum Corda,* the priest reads the Preface silently, only the closing phrase, mentioning Cherubim and Seraphim, being said aloud. After the *Sanctus* there is a solemn *Sanctus* Prayer. During the Preface and *Sanctus* Prayer the Armenian priest lifts up his outspread hands; at the words "Cherubim and Seraphim" he holds his hands one above the other over the chalice, as does the Latin priest at the *Hanc Igitur.*

10. Before the consecration the priest lays the host on his left hand and blesses it, and extends his arms somewhat, looking up to heaven. For the remainder the manner of Consecration is like the Latin, except for the elevation, which takes place later, after the Our Father.

11. At the elevation of the Sacred Species there is a prayer of praise to the Holy Trinity. Before setting down the chalice, the priest reverently kisses its foot.

12. Especially effective is the sacramental blessing with the chalice, and the sacred Host held over it. This is at once an invitation and a warning to receive the sacred Body of the Lord in holiness: "He is Life and Hope of Resurrection and Forgiveness of Sins; He is our King!" (The priest then makes a complete turn about.)

13. The particle of the Host is placed in the chalice entirely after the Latin manner; there is no "signing" of the Host with the precious Blood.

14. The Last Gospel (John 1) is read solemnly in exactly the same manner as the first.

15. At the words "Peace be to all" and at the end of the Mass the priest gives the blessing in the Roman fashion.

16. The broad collar standing up above the Mass vestment is a distinctive sign of the Armenian priest.

17. Armenian churches usually have two curtains: a big one between sanctuary and nave, and a small one before the altar. During Mass on feast days the larger curtain is drawn closed twice: from the introductory prayer till the Introit, and after the distribution of Communion till the Last Gospel; the smaller is drawn closed only once: from the fraction until the Communion of the faithful.

18. At solemn liturgies, *flabella* are used. These are staves about six feet in length, bearing at one end a metal plaque with the representation of a cherub, and with small bells hung round the edges. They are carried, waving gently, at the head of the procession round the altar with Gospel book and bread and wine; they are shaken so as to ring the bells at the Trisagion and at the Lord's Prayer.

ON GOING UP TO THE ALTAR

"In the House of Holiness and the place of praise, in this dwelling of angels and sanctuary of atonement of all men, we do prostrate ourselves in awe and reverence, and do worship before these tokens, well-pleasing to God, and before this Holy Altar. We laud and praise Thy Holy, Wonderful, and Victorious Resurrection; and we offer unto Thee as well as to the Father and the Holy Ghost, praise and honor, now and ever and unto ages of ages. Amen."

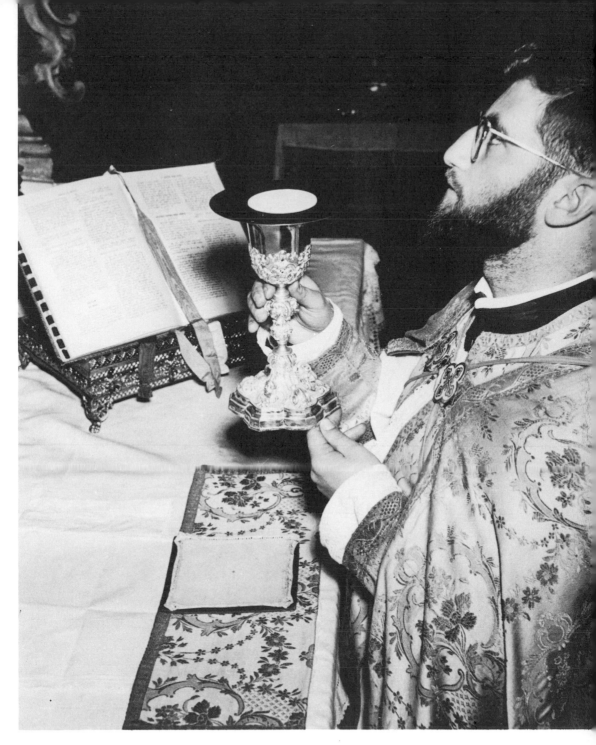

OFFERTORY

"Be mindful, O Gracious Lover of Men, of those who offer now to Thee and of those for whom they offer; and as for us, do Thou preserve us faultless in the priestly administration of Thy Divine Mysteries; for holy and glorious is the most venerable majesty of the glory of the Father and the Son and the Holy Ghost, now and ever and unto ages of ages. Amen."

GOSPEL

The priest blesses the faithful with the Gospel book and reads the Gospel, the server standing meanwhile at his right with a burning candle. Then he prays: "Falling down before God, let us praise the Holy Trinity, which was before all eternity, and the One Godhead of the Father and of the Son and of the Holy Ghost, now and ever and unto ages of ages. Amen."

162

THE SANCTUS PRAYER

"Holy, holy, holy, art Thou in very truth, and holier than all else that is. Who can boast himself in words to comprehend in words the outpouring of Thine immeasurable goodness? For behold, Thou hast, from the beginning, kept watch over man who had fallen into sin; and hast comforted him in manifold and divers fashions. . . . In the latter days hast Thou torn up the writ of our condemnation for all our sins and hast given us Thy Son, as debtor and debt, as Victim and Anointed, as Lamb and Bread from Heaven, as High Priest and Sacrifice."

163

CONSECRATION

"When He had taken the Bread into His holy, divine, spotless, Creator's hands, He blessed it; and when He had given thanks, broke it, and gave it to His chosen Holy Apostles, who sat with Him at table, saying: 'Take and eat; this is My Body which is given for you and for many, for the expiation and forgiveness of sins.'"

PRAYER AFTER CONSECRATION

"Yea, verily, we praise Thee, O Lord Our God, and we thank without ceasing, that Thou hast deigned to make us, notwithstanding our own unworthiness, ministers of such a dread and ineffable mystery. Not trusting in our own merits, but in Thine exceeding goodness, do we presume to draw near to the ministration of the Body and Blood of Thine Only-Begotten Son, Jesus Christ. To Him belongeth glory, power, and honor, now and ever and unto ages of ages. Amen."

ELEVATION OF THE SACRED SPECIES

At the elevation of the sacred Host: "Holy Things for the Holy! Blessed art Thou, O Holy One, very God and Father! Blessed art Thou, the Son, Holy and very God! Blessed art Thou, O Holy Ghost, very God!"

At the elevation of the chalice: "Look down upon us, O Lord, from Thy Heaven on high; come, sanctify and save us."

PRAYER OF THE BLESSING AFTER LAST GOSPEL

First the priest reads, with great solemnity, the Last Gospel: "In the beginning was the Word. . . ."

Thereafter, he closes the book, and before giving the blessing, says the prayer of the blessing, ending with the words: "Be ye all blessed by the grace of the Holy Ghost. Go in peace!"

ARMENIAN PONTIFICAL IN THE SISTINE CHAPEL
IN PRESENCE OF THE POPE

ELEVATION OF SACRED SPECIES AFTER THE LORD'S PRAYER

"Blessed art Thou, O Holy Father, true God. Amen.

"Blessed art Thou, O Holy Son, true God. Amen.

"Blessed art Thou, O Holy Ghost, true God. Amen.

"Praise and honor be to Father and Son and Holy Ghost now and always from eternity to eternity. Amen.

"Look down upon us, O Lord Jesus Christ, from heaven, from Thy holy place, and from the glorious throne of Thy Kingdom; come to sanctify us and to give us life, Thou who art enthroned with the Father, and offered here; vouchsafe to make us, and through our ministry, all this people, partakers of Thy spotless Body and of Thy precious Blood."